The Butcher of Lyon

by

MANUEL LASSO

This is a work of fiction. Names, characters, places, and actions are the product of the imagination and invention of the author. Any resemblance or similarity to actual persons, living or deceased, events, places or actions is completely coincidental.

DEDICATION

To Mila, my wife, with unending love.

ACKNOWLEDGMENTS

Special thanks to my son John for helping me in the edition of this work, to my daughter Kathleen for her guidance in finding the best way to print it and to my son Michael for assisting me in the legal aspects of this publication.

1

A TORTURED FRENCHMAN

"He tortured me at the *E'Cole de Santé Militaire, monsieur*, on the other side of the Rhône, across from the Terminus Hotel. The first day, I was left alone with him in a large warehouse. We could hear the music of Wagner, *Die Walküre... Musique merveilleuse, monsieur...* I remember Gerhilde singing... *Heiaha!... Ho-jo-te-jo!...* The lieutenant was standing in the distance, almost hidden in the darkness, with his black uniform, wearing a red band with a swastika on his left arm. He was very calm, almost in meditation, holding a nightstick in his hands. The shadows didn't allow me to see the details of his face. At first, he didn't do anything and remained quiet, listening to the music. Worriedly, I continued looking at his silhouette, *monsieur,* and wondered when he would begin to interrogate me. Suddenly, while the *Valkyiries* sang... *Haya-yoho... Haya-yoho!,* he sprinted towards me as if I was escaping. This was something I didn't understand. When he got close, *monsieur*, he battered me with his stick and I felt the most terrible pain all over my head. I thought my skull had exploded into pieces. I remember his fine leather gloves. He didn't ask me anything. He only beat me and beat me. He must have been in excellent physical

1

shape because he hit me rapidly and tirelessly. His movements were impeccable and exact. He knew where to land his blows. He didn't get weary or short of breath. The lieutenant struck me on my neck, my arms and my back. When I covered my head, he smashed me below. When I protected my private parts, he pounded me on my ear and I had a terrible buzzing sensation and the feeling that my head had burst. He did everything with perfection and great coordination, with elegant movements, as if he had rehearsed innumerable times. I was stooping from the horrible pain. Little by little, my body began to bend. I felt that my legs were giving up and I passed out, *monsieur*. When I woke up, I was on the floor, face down, slightly nauseated. The music of the *Valkyries* continued magnificently. It was the Third Act, when the heroines are gathering the soldiers' bodies. I saw the tips of his well-shined boots and felt the strong smell of the shoe polish. He had his assistants pick me up and looked at me with a great calmness as if calculating my remaining strength. Then, *monsieur*, he struck me again with the same elegance and eagerness as the first time, on my head, on my neck and on my back. He didn't interrogate me at all. He only banged me with his nightstick on all sides. He ordered his assistants to hit me together with him. He called Goulé Tordué and they beat me more violently. Once, while they were all punishing me, he exclaimed furiously something that until now I remember very clearly: *"Ein Führer, ein volk, ein stat!"* (One leader, one people, one state!) Then all of them battered me with more exaltation as if they were performing God's will. My knees buckled, collapsing immediately, and I lost consciousness. They immersed me in a tub filled with freezing water. When I woke up, I felt the icy water entering my nostrils. I was suffocating. They pulled me out of the tub coughing, shivering violently and my teeth chattering. I thought I was going to die and almost let myself drop to the floor. They dried me off quickly; but almost immediately, they hurt me again. This brutal martyrdom lasted for seven

2

days during which no one asked me anything. Only at the end, after tormenting me so sadistically, when my ears were droning loudly and I could not open my eyes because they were puffed up and when I was so weak that I did not know if I was dead or alive, he asked me one single question. Coming close to me, with a very soft and serene voice, almost whispering, he asked me: "Who is Didier?" I looked at him with absolute astonishment. I didn't know who that person was. I saw the white *S.D.* letters of his black neck collar, his amicable and compassionate eyes and his smiling lips. I answered: "I don't know... I do not know him." Surprised he asked me again. "You don't know him?" "No. I don't." He became angry; but remained silent for a moment. Once he calmed down, he said to his men. "He doesn't know... *Leben Und leben lasse!*" (Live and let live!) He ordered them to abandon me at the outskirts of Lyon. They left me reclining, with my arms open, over the long row of stone seats of the Romain Ampithéâtre, with a sheet of paper attached to my chest by a safety pin, which said. "*Il ne sait pas.*" (He doesn't know.)

2

THE CAPTURE OF LYON

The *Wehrmacht* soldiers, with sharp daggers in their scabbards, and round canteens full of water hanging from their shoulders, screamed *"Vorwärts, immer vorwärts!"* (Forward, always forward!), and ran towards the Royal Hotel at the Place Bellecour of Lyon. They occupied it with the same efficiency as they captured the Arch of Triumph, in Paris.

Hours later endless platoons of young Nazi soldiers, still adolescents, with letters from their mothers in their pockets, carrying big flame-throwers on their backs, marched orderly in front of an anxious Lyonnais crowd standing along the *rue de la Barre*. Some of the soldiers, the older ones, passed by on their roaring motorcycles. They had dusty faces and binoculars around their necks. A well-groomed, 5 year old French boy, holding a small black flag, shot at one of them with his finger. "Bang, bang, bang!" The German soldier slowed down, calmly turned around his trembling *BMW R75* motorcycle, supporting himself with an extended foot and came back expelling the annoying smell of its *750 cc* engine fumes. After realizing that it was only a child who was shooting at him with his little index finger, the soldier smiled and said: *"Netter Junge!"* (Nice kid!) He revved the right-hand throttle of his vehicle and continued his journey together with the other thunderous motorcycles.

The combatants of the German infantry division went through the streets of Lyon, with rifles on their shoulders, marching with resounding steps over the cobblestone road, to the musical beat of the *Blitzkrieg* military march. They followed the artillery guns, covered by dirty brown nets and pulled forward by a large number of disciplined and obedient Nazi mules.

With their constantly rolling caterpillar tracks, the armored Tiger I tanks emerged suddenly, slowly turning their heavy **88** mm cannons to one side and then to the other. They raised them and lowered them, aiming at the crowds, who protested against this provocative action with shrills and acidic comments. They also pointed their guns at the towers of the *Fourvière Basilica* and at the Roman Amphytheatre. There were tanks everywhere, moving in all directions. For a moment, it seemed that all the *Panzer* tanks of Nazi Germany had congregated in the city of Lyon.

The soldiers, with heavy *M-42* helmets and leather thongs tightly buckled under their chins, brought large amount of *Mausermunition* cartridges, in wooden boxes, and placed them over the stone pavement. Quickly the German officers secured the access to the bridges of the Saône River and the Rhône River placing tanks at the entrance of each one and machine guns with tripods and belt-fed ammunition of 150 rounds each at the shores. The inhabitants of Lyon could not do anything about the occupation. It had occurred without their consent and they expressed their dissatisfaction in a symbolic way. When the German soldiers marched in front of them, singing the *Horst Wessel*, and lifting their boots as high as they could, the civilians turned around and showed them their backs.

During those days, something peculiar and unforgettable happened at the Place Bellecour. A young

Werhmacht soldier stopped in front of the Louis XIV monument and clicked his heels. Gallantly, he raised his right arm and observed the laurel crown and the short sword of the statue of the French King, represented as a Roman Emperor. He glanced at the sandals and the tunic of the statue, the muscular leg of the horse and its thick mane. Softly, the young combatant sang the first strophe of the *Horst Wessel*. With his *G43* rifle on his shoulder and a long stick grenade tucked into his belt, looking at the green statue with reverence, he continued with the second strophe, almost without moving his lips and keeping his heels together. At that moment, a bomb placed by a member of the French Resistance, exploded with a thunderous sound and the German soldier flew into small pieces. Everyone saw his fragments and his helmet flying from an immense yellow fireball. They observed, through the white smoke, the bits of his green bluish uniform falling slowly over the stone pavement.

Immediately an *S.S.* officer gave an order and several soldiers went running through the streets and arrested the first twenty pedestrians they found. The soldiers shoved these unwarned citizens with their hands up, until they were in front of the Louis XIV monument. Then, the soldiers shot them with their submachine guns. They transformed the twenty prisoners into a heap of bodies, at the same place where the young soldier had tried to sing the *Horst Wessel*.

At dawn, the troops captured the Terminus Hotel. Screaming repeatedly *"Sturm Lyon!"* ("Attack Lyon!") and holding their shiny *Schmeisser* submachine guns, they took it by surprise, as if they were carrying out another *Blitzkrieg* in Poland, although there was no one armed inside, not even with a safety pin. Very swiftly, they occupied the *foyer* of the hotel pointing their guns at the occupants. A rumbling 1931 motorcycle with a sidecar entered the hall and made several rounds with great clatter. After stopping, an *S.D.* lieutenant descended from the vehicle. He stumbled and limped a little for a few seconds. Then he remained standing and looking at everybody. The terrified employees raised their hands and remained quiet.

The Terminus Hotel had an impressive XIX century appearance. It was decorated with a style similar to the *Belle Époque*. It had panels, mirrors and erotic Pompeian frescos, covering its walls. The handrails of the elegant stairway were brightly polished and the light of the candelabra illuminated the burnished black boots of the soldiers who climbed over the carpeted steps. There was always, in the *foyer,* a chamber orchestra with lecterns and musical scores playing melodies of Strauss, Vivaldi or Verdi. On that particular occasion, they played the *Brandenburg Concerto No. 6* by Bach.

From the hotel windows, it was possible to see the *Cours* of *Verdun* and the busy train station of *Perrache* with its green cars and black locomotives with golden ornaments, whistling intermittently and releasing soot and black smoke from their chimneys. At the Terminus Hotel, the Gestapo established its general headquarters.

Surprisingly someone had already placed an enormous red flag with a black *hakenkreus* (swastika) within a white circle on the ceiling of the main lobby. Also, somebody had been diligent enough to play a record on the front desk phonograph and unexpectedly the rumbling voice of Hitler resounded through the loudspeakers, with an echo, delivering one of his Berlin speeches.

The lieutenant, with his new leather gloves, moved slowly paying attention to the allocution. Short and robust, he wore a black leather overcoat, so long that at moments it seemed to be touching the floor. On his belt, he carried a *Welther Pistolen P38.* His cap had a party ensign and a black visor with no ornaments. Cold and disdainful, he wanted to give the impression that he was one of the generals of the Third Reich, someone like Martin Bormann or Rudolf Hess, listening to his leader. When the vehement peroration ended, he searched the entire building for a space that could serve him as an office. He found one on the third floor. It was room 68.

Upon entering the chamber, the lieutenant perceived a delightful perfume and observed in the shiny mirror on the ceiling, the reflection of his own image and those of his men. He ordered the removal of all the furniture and his men went in and out taking things until the room became empty. The lieutenant pointed to a porcelain chamber pot left in the center of the room and someone fetched it and took it away. Then he ordered to take down the dirty curtains and the old panels. Raising dust, they also removed the mirrors from the walls. His men carried in a walnut desk and several chairs, together with black inkwells, pens and a pink blotter. They also brought stamps with black round handles, two flogs and a pair of electrical wires.

Advancing with quick and short steps, four men arrived holding an immense oil painting of Hitler, so big and heavy that it seemed to be falling out of their hands. Raising the visor of his cap, the lieutenant ordered to hang it behind his desk. On the large portrait, the *Führer* appeared in Party brown uniform with a swastika on one arm, a tuft of black hair falling over his forehead and a hand scratching his waist.

Later on, the lieutenant ordered to place more sepia and black and white photographs of Hitler, in all sizes and poses, in all the rooms and corridors of the Terminus Hotel. It was imperative to have him present at all times. The soldiers even hung them in the bathrooms, above the washbasins, the toilets and the paper rolls. They stayed there for a long time until one morning the pictures of the *Führer* appeared soiled. Apparently, someone had scribbled on them the words *"Heil Hitler!"* Alarmed the lieutenant decided to remove them from the bathrooms. The soldiers cleaned them and hung them in other places, where nobody could touch them.

During those days, there were rumors that one of the Panzer tanks of the Saône River Bridge had appeared with a black swastika drawn on one side of the turret. No one saw anybody and no one knew how this occurred; but everybody was convinced that it was the work of a daring member of the French Resistance. Fearful that someone would stain the big portrait of Hitler, the lieutenant ordered that a guard should stay in his office at all times.

During that weekend, the young *teuton* who was guarding the painting got up from his chair, removed his helmet and accommodated the rifle butt on his shoulder aiming at the face of the *Führer*. He closed one eye and with the other he focused on the black moustache and the small shiny reflection in one of Hitler's eyes. He remained in that position for a few moments. Then slowly he lowered the rifle and sat down on the big leather chair of the lieutenant. With greasy fingers, he continued eating his burnt pale *Fränkische bratwurst* with *sauerkraut*.

3

ODETTE

After the sunset, the Gestapo and the *Wehrmacht* officers entertained themselves at the numerous nightclubs of the city and at the parties given by the Royal Hotel, the Bristol and the Terminus. These social gatherings were very entertaining. Everybody drank excessively as good Germans and danced very happily until late. The rich owners of the hotels provided the officers with beautiful and elegant French women that left them exhausted. These holidays had no ending. Some wished to continue day and night; but military obligations forced them to return to their barracks and offices.

The night Odette came they were all drunk, grotesquely dancing to the joyous Bavarian music with very catchy melodies. Hans Schultz was the happiest of all. He had promised to make love with all the gentle women present after dancing with them. He already had ten on his account. With his reddened face, all elated by the vigor of youth and his blond hair falling over his forehead, he passed by very happily dancing the *So Ein Tag*.

Klaus was the most quiet. He was peacefully standing, next to the curtains, with a glass of champagne in his hand, looking at the other celebrants. Concerned by the general drunkenness he feared that if a squad of maquis could enter the ballroom at that moment, they could shoot them all, with their British machine guns. Then the Gestapo would have to make hustled interments in the cemetery and bring replacements from Paris and Berlin immediately. Afterwards he thought about the wife he had left in Munich and felt immensely nostalgic, until Hans Schultz approached him and with his drunken eyes introduced him to Odette. The intensity of the music played by the band and the voices of the singing officers did not allow him to hear well. Bringing one ear close to her lips, very respectfully, he asked again for her name. Both laughed with unexpected animation.

Odette was a beautiful French woman with brown eyes. She was dazzling. She had two round buns of black hair on her head and wore a white dress with pink flowery designs and shoulder pads. Smiling, she invited him to dance. To the rhythm of the brass and on the beat of the percussionist, he started taking steps laterally dancing the *Rosamunde*:

> *"Ich bin schon seit Tagen*
> *verliebt in Rosamunde.*
> *Ich denke jede Stunde,*
> *sie muß es erfahren.*
> *Seh ich ihre Lippen*
> *mit dem frohen Lachen,*
> *möcht ich alles wagen,*
> *um sie mal zu küssen."*

They danced through many songs. The polkas and the Bavarian waltzes played continuously. The applauses and hisses were endless. She could not stop smiling at him. Odette praised the way he danced. Without knowing what to say, he nodded his head and kept slapping his thighs, knees and feet. Up to that moment, he only wanted to be a good *S.D.* officer and tried to think exclusively of his wife; but when he saw the happy eyes of Odette and her captivating smile, he did not wish to think about anyone else. Whenever she came near and he felt her warmness, he lost all his will. At that moment and only at that moment she could have done with him whatever she wanted. After dancing several songs and making several turns around the dance floor, among drunken officers who had fallen unconscious over their chairs, he did not want to do anything else, but to keep gliding with Odette. He forgot about the wife who was waiting for him with a steaming plate of *Pichelsteiner* at the quiet table of her remote Bavaria. Soon he became addicted to Odette's smile. He did not want to do anything else, but to see her gleaming. After the tenth *polka,* she asked him to take her to the balcony in search of fresh air. He embraced her on their way out and they passed by a gray haired Colonel who was sluggishly resting in a chair lifting one hand with dull movements and giving an unintelligible speech, in a laughable imitation of Hitler, on the extermination of the non-Aryan race from the surface of the earth.

Once outside, while enjoying the breeze, she asked him if he would like to go on Sunday to the *Cathédrale Saint-Jean-Baptiste,* to see the astronomical clock with the moving figures of the Annunciation and the bugle player. However, he could not pay attention to her words anymore because her nearness had transformed him into a catapulting beast and hugged her tighter. She asked him. "What are you doing, darling?" He kissed her on the face, on the neck and on the hands. "No, please. Not here," she said closing her eyes and letting him caress her. "What are you doing, my love... What are you doing?"

Odette worked on the first floor of the Terminus Hotel. She was the secretary of Colonel Fritz Harteck. Klaus had never noticed her; but she felt strongly attracted to him from the first time she saw him talking to Harteck and dreamed of meeting him. The following week she moved to Klaus's office and started working as his secretary.

4

OYONNAX

The liberation of Oyonnax by the French Resistance took place at the beginning of November. It was a symbolic act, not a real emancipation. It was a challenge to the Gestapo and it took effect under the leadership of the Mayor, who was the chief of the maquis from Ain. He was a decorated First World War hero and knew everything about trench battles, the hair-raising terror felt during the bombings of the heavy German artillery and the panic caused by a sudden attack with mustard gas. He understood that a big deal of courage was necessary in order to leave a trench, to confront the enemy, only with a *Berthier* rifle and an old bayonet. That day, in order to raise the morale of the members of the Resistance, he announced an assembly to give a speech on the invincibility myth of the Nazi soldiers.

While getting dressed, he opened his wardrobe and immediately, in his mind, he heard shots on a cloudy morning and remembered one of his wounded comrades with his muddy overcoat slowly sliding into a trench. He paused for a moment and then put on the blue jacket and the red breeches he had worn as an infantry captain, in the battle of Verdun. Afterwards, he put on a blue kepi with golden designs, with a flat-topped crown, and a horizontal visor. He placed an M2 anti gas mask around his neck and unwillingly he remembered the night when he had to evacuate his trench because it became flooded by a slowly moving greenish gas. On his blue jacket, he pinned a polished bronze medal showing the image of a French soldier with the phrase "*On ne passe pas.*" ("They will not pass.")

When his men saw him putting his white gloves on, they had the feeling that a scene from the glorious past had reappeared in front of them. Then the Mayor mounted on a motorcycle that his men had snatched recently from the young soldiers of Colonel Harteck. Riding slowly, in the middle of a thunderous noise, he advanced through the streets of Oyonnax, followed by his maquis, who were proudly showing their new British machine guns. They left a crown of flowers at the main square in honor of the heroes who had fallen defending France. Surprisingly, the Nazis were eating *jagerschnitzels* at a nearby place, sitting under the shadow of the trees, a few blocks away.

For the villagers this was something unbelievable because it was an open challenge to the *Wehrmacht*. The curious neighbors became very enthusiastic and soon the entire town was celebrating the liberation of Oyonnax. The multitude went mad and sang the *Marseillaise*. There was an instant and immense happiness. The villagers sang and cried; they embraced each other. They asked if the Germans had already left. The Mayor, slowly caressing his white moustache, assuredly said: "They are not gone yet; but we will make them leave soon." The townspeople applauded until their hands hurt. Then they heard shots of machine guns in the distance. The Mayor, with his blue-red uniform and his anti-gas mask on his chest, sat up straight on his motorcycle, smelling the danger, and inflated his chest. It seemed to him that he was back to that rainy day, at the battle of Verdun, when he had to advance the French line, moving over the mud, throwing his grenades and expecting to enter in hand-to-hand combat at any moment. He raised his arm, pointed exactly to the place where the shots were coming from and exclaimed:

"*J'attaque!*" Increasing the speed of his rumbling engine, he moved forward followed by his men.

It was never known where they went; but from that instant the confidence of the maquis raised considerably. They began seeing the German invaders as mere mortals who could be defeated. It was not a military victory, but an emancipation of the spirit.

5

IN THE TORTURE CHAMBER

Odette visited Klaus throughout the day even during the torture sessions. Smiling, with a floral dress, she used to come at lunchtime, exactly at twelve noon. She entered walking briskly, clunking sharply with the high heels of her red shoes. She liked to carry a metallic tray with ham sandwiches and a glass of beer, covered by multicolored napkins. Sometimes she would only bring sardines dipped in oil and crackers. She entered, gazing at him with passion. She would not take her half-closed eyes off him.

That day she looked at him the same way she did the first time she saw him. She remembered Klaus entering Colonel Fritz Harteck's office in a hurry, asking him to sign a letter addressed to the high command in Berlin. Presumptuously, he requested his promotion to Captain. Claiming that he had sent enough prisoners to Auschwitz and Birkenau, he thought he deserved a reward. Colonel Harteck, with a monocle in one eye, read the letter and shook his head disapprovingly. Looking coldly at the lieutenant, he said. "You have to send more prisoners, Klaus. Ten times as many. You have not done enough. The high command will laugh at this request." Klaus seemed like a disconsolate child. That was what Odette remembered. At the same time, she thought that the lieutenant was the most handsome man on earth. She had never seen a more gorgeous officer in all her life. Where in heaven had this man been before? At that moment, she swore to herself to make all efforts to meet him. She was just captivated by him. No one could do anything about it.

When she brought lunch, she flirted with him. It was beyond her will. She enjoyed playing *Rosamunde* on the phonograph. Then, she lowered the volume and came close to him again. While he was giving orders to his assistants from his chair, she fed him pieces of a sandwich and gave him a sip of beer.

It was obvious that she was terribly in love with him. She would sit down on his lap and rubbed herself softly against his thighs. She said to him while caressing his cheek, "*Mon amour*. Why didn't you come last night? I couldn't stand being without you. I was going crazy, crazy, really crazy."

It was true. When he failed to see her at night, terrible thoughts came to her mind. The most pernicious was the idea that he was with another woman. This made her very angry. Crossing her arms, walking back and forth inside her bedroom, she hated the other woman. She wondered who it was. She remembered a blond woman with a black veil and little swastikas embroidered on her nylon stocks, who came to see Colonel Harteck two days before. She came asking for a relative, but at the end, she asked for Klaus. Perhaps, Odette thought, it was another young woman, the one who came with her father, to request a pass to go to Paris. However, she could not take her eyes away from Klaus, who was writing at a nearby desk. Odette bit her lips with irritation, while those evil thoughts tortured her. Or perhaps, it was his gray-haired wife who had come to visit him? Furiously, she banged the wall with her two small fists. Then, she rubbed her face, ruining her make-up and her hairdo. She sat down on a chair and sobbed angrily thinking that Klaus could be kissing another woman at that precise moment.

When she came to see Klaus, she would tell him with a sad face.

"I can't take you out of my mind, *mon amour*. No matter how hard I try, I can't do it. Wherever I go, your image comes with me and appears in my mind. You don't know how much I love you. You don't know how much I miss you."

He embraced her tightly; but at the same time, he continued interrogating the prisoner while his aids beat him hard. The screams of the naked prisoner, tied to the table, were loud. At times, it seemed like an unending howling. However, Odette was not aware of Klaus' assistants or their actions. For her, they did not exist. All her attention was concentrated in passing her fingers over his shaved face, looking at his green eyes. She could not resist. How handsome he seemed to her.

She enjoyed feeding him and letting him sip from the glass of beer, while pressing her legs against his knees. She became warm and felt like she was in a trance. Then, still looking at him with desire, she slowly wiped his mouth with the multicolored napkin and brought her face close to his.

They kissed while the men tortured the prisoner. She playfully touched his thighs with her fingers. Giggling, she put her hand over his soft crotch and squeezed hard. For a moment, he stopped paying attention to his helpers and absorbed himself on what she was doing. Smiling she opened his pants, saying:

"You have no will, *mon amour*. You are completely mine now."

Almost out of her mind, she lifted her creamy floral dress and sat over his thighs, facing him. It was something beyond her control. She began moving slowly while closing her eyes. Klaus distracted himself by singing, almost without moving his lips:

"*Die Fahne hoch...*"

He kissed her and hugged her. With his strong hand, he caressed her back and shoulders, looking at the cuff of his black jacket. Odette opened her blouse and exposed her splendid bosoms. While she held his face with her hands, he gently kissed her without thinking about his men anymore. She kept moving slowly. It was a hot day in Lyon, lunchtime.

"*die Reihen fest geschlossen...*"

She rocked over him, faster and faster, with more energy, breathing fast and saying:

"*Je t'aime, mon amour... Je t'aime...*"

He saw the small drops of perspiration appear on her forehead. He sensed the perfumed smell that came off her body and found it most enjoyable. Moving with more energy, she seemed to be galloping and panting. She moaned loudly, swinging her head up and down, murmuring:

"Hold it, my love, hold it. Please."

He spoke in German while kissing her pearly bosoms with his eyes closed:

"*Kraft durch freude!*" (Strength through joy!)

Suddenly they became quiet. Both of them were perspiring and breathing fast. His concerned assistant had called him. Klaus shoved her away gently. She dismounted and remained standing, blushing and perspiring. She stared at the floor and passed a hand through her hair.

He looked at his helpers worriedly, trying to understand what had happened. It seemed to him that he had awakened from a dream. He stood up, straightening his uniform and became serious. He cleared his throat.

"*Führer*," said his assistant. "The prisoner does not respond..."

"What?" he asked with irritation, still fixing his pants.

"He doesn't react anymore, *Führer*."

There was a moment of silence; then Klaus laughed frantically.

"You hit him too hard, stupid!" he said while putting his arm around Odette's shoulders.

He laughed and laughed. He could not stop laughing. Then they walked towards the door. Before leaving, he gave his final instruction.

"Throw him in the Saône River. No, no! Wait! Throw him in the Rhône. It will be better."

"Why in the Rhône, sir?"

"Because the Romans used to throw the ashes of the Christian martyrs in the Rhône River, *Leerer Kopf!* (Empty head!)"

On their way to her apartment, he continued laughing and commenting about what happened.

6

COLONEL FRITZ HARTECK

What bothered Colonel Harteck the most were the numerous reports indicating that the maquis from Oyonnax were everywhere, bragging about their new and shiny British submachine guns. They enjoyed showing them to the young women as well as to the elderly citizens of town, who enjoyed sharing many wine bottles with the members of the French Resistance. They were also destroying the railroad tracks whenever they wanted, on the hills, on the outskirts of town and even near the railroad stations. They were blowing up the tracks in front of curious crowds, which roared and clapped, celebrating the achievements of the Resistance. No one could find them or capture them, not even by search dogs or by tanks, which rolled through the streets threatening everybody with their heavy cannons. The French Resistance was becoming a demonic force that continued defying the Gestapo and the *Werhmacht*. For a moment, Colonel Fritz Harteck had the frightening idea that everything was an act of pure and simple witchcraft.

A special train, he had sent to Paris carrying one hundred Auschwitz-bound prisoners was captured by the maquis, who liberated the detainees and advised them to disappear. The Nazi guards had to drop their guns and abandon the train to stand in perfect formation by the side of the cars. While the locomotive was whistling and releasing steam, the maquis made them pull out their handkerchiefs and wave goodbye to them. Afterward, from side to side, they shot them with their submachine guns.

When Colonel Harteck arrived, wearing all the medals he received for his heroic actions in Belgium, the train was gone. All he could see were his dead teenage soldiers, lying along the tracks, still with their white handkerchiefs in their hands. "This is impossible!" he exclaimed horrified. "How could this ever happen when *Herr der Lage sein?* (We are the masters of the situation?) This is a challenge to our *Führergott*, an insult to our race and an affront to the Third Reich!" He never heard again from the special train that the maquis had removed from the area. The captives escaped, running over the beets and cabbages of the countryside and vanished as if by magic or witchery.

Every time Colonel Harteck sent a patrol of young recruits to capture a maqui, to the Saint-Jean area or to the hilly Croix-Rousse, they all ended up dead or at least very badly wounded. When these Nazi soldiers found a suspect in these neighborhoods and asked him to stop, the maqui would turn the corner waving good-bye and would disappear as if by a clear act of incantation. If the *S.S.* soldiers dared to enter through the *traboules,* they appeared on the other end with their own daggers interred in their bellies or with their throats sliced. Occasionally, they would appear completely mangled by one of their own stick grenades. Now and then, if a Nazi soldier would dare to ride his motorcycle through these areas, the rider would vanish and the machine would keep rolling down the hill. It was a *non-plus ultra* for the German soldiers.

The Colonel concluded that everything was happening as Nostradamus had predicted. He would have to send a complete Panzer division to the Ain forests to exterminate the entire civilian population, guilty or innocent, in order to end these acts of sorcery.

Only killing everyone, he could be sure that the members of the French Resistance had also died.

He asked the help of General Hans Herbert Auerbach, who before the war had made his living as a magician, a mentalist and an escapist of a circus. Always surrounded by elephants, tigers and clowns, the press called him the *Fakir of Berlin*. Nevertheless, the General told Colonel Harteck that although he agreed with the idea of eliminating the maquis, surrounding them with a huge army in order to choke them, he was not in the position to send an entire Panzer division to the forests of Ain. The reason being that some of his soldiers were old reservists who spent their time calculating in a notebook the amount of money they would receive during their retirement. They only thought of finishing the war as soon as possible, to return to the motherland and live in peace for the rest of their existence.

He also said that his other soldiers were members of the Hitlerian Youth, aroused by patriotism, but did not know how to use their rifles. They were only good for distributing cyanide capsules among those who did not believe in the doctrines of the National Socialism. They spent their days asking General Auerbach to teach them his secrets to swallow a saber without feeling any pain and without choking. They were obsessively curious about his technique to get rid of chains and shackles. Unfortunately, they could neither load their weapons properly, nor shoot the enemy with them. Besides, they did not have any experience in guerrilla warfare. All they talked about was their mothers, the chemical composition of cyanide and the way the pharmaceutical companies manufactured these capsules. The General told Colonel Harteck about the fears he had that the maquis could massacre an entire division in a matter of seconds. These young men were not at the level of the saboteurs. He asked the Colonel to have patience, because before giving any response, he had to consult with his superiors in Berlin.

At that moment, without asking for any authorization, the resented Colonel Harteck, with his reddened face, ordered one hundred young soldiers of General Hans Herbert Auerbach to go to Nantua and arrest the first fifty men they could find. It took the entire day for the soldiers to go from house to house, shooting indiscriminately at any target with their machine guns, which seemed to be falling out of their hands. They went around breaking doors and dragging people out of their houses. Before sunset, they had captured the fifty men.

Then, the Colonel ordered to hang big white signs with black skulls on the trees along the roads indicating that the Gestapo would not tolerate symbolic acts of rebellion that were dishonoring the German Army. They also banned curses and enchantments and hung signs everywhere bearing the statement "Witchery is forbidden" or "Black Magic is not allowed." When the maquis found these signs on the trees they shattered them with their machine guns and ran away laughing unendingly.

Before initiating the retreat of his troops toward the Ardennes, Colonel Fritz Harteck, had an extraordinary idea with which he thought he could give the final blow to the Resistance. He called the members of his *Einsatzkommando* and ordered them to capture the Mayor of Oyonnax. They were to bring him alive, wearing his blue captain jacket and red pantaloon, including his polished bronze medal and his motorcycle. The diligent, although young soldiers, went to the woods and looked for the municipal authority throughout the entire countryside without any luck. Shooting in the air, they entered the houses of the farmers; but did not find anybody. With their almost infantile voices, they blindly opened fire at the straw stacks and the poultry-yards, raising dust and feathers and making the white chickens run away. Nevertheless, they had no better luck. They advanced by the shores of the rivers, sometimes stumbling on them, firing their weapons against the stones and the surface of the streams of clean water.

However they did not find the Mayor of Oyonnax or his WWI French blue jacket and red breeches either. Following the aroma of a recently baked ham with clover sticks, they arrived at the cabin of a horticulturist; but they did not find any municipal authority. Only after several local maidens informed them that the mayor had gone to the mountains of Ain to pick up wine barrels and to reorganize his militias, the young soldiers changed their purpose and agreed to do something different.

They enjoyed the smell of the warm *Tart aux pommes* the young women offered to them. As a sign of appreciation one of the beardless youths, with the snapping of a finger, made a red rose appear in front of the face of the astounded young woman and gave it to her with a sudden click of his heels and a deep reverence. Then they entered the shack and played *So Ein Tag* on the phonograph. The lads left their submachine guns leaning against the rustic walls and danced with the young women. Like in a fairy tale, they cheerfully moved in circles until the music stopped.

As if waking up from a deep and wonderful dream the soldiers left the girls, grabbed their weapons and came out of the house as fast as they could in search of the Mayor, screaming with their childish voices: "*Stürm Oyonnax! Stürm Oyonnax!*" (Attack Oyonnax!) After a deeper search in the forest, they found the citizen who was replacing the Mayor, resting in front of his stove, with his hands holding an old cane. Only when they took him out to the open field, they realized that the elderly wine maker was blind. They also arrested Mr. Delestraint, a cheese merchant from Tolouse, who had come to visit him. The young soldiers did not ask for their names. They placed them under the shadow of a leafy tree and in the name of the National Socialism and the Third Reich they fired at them. Then they carried the warm bodies to the town square and placed them delicately over the dry flowers that the Mayor of Oyonnax had left several days earlier, during the town liberation. Clicking their heels, they saluted, raised their arms, and left.

At that moment, Colonel Harteck, was frustrated trying to obtain an entire *Wehrmacht* division from General Auerbach. While Fritz Harteck was speaking, the General, who for many years had worked as a mentalist and an escapist in a Berlin circus, showed him a pair of new and shiny handcuffs and said. "Put them on. I will teach you how to get out of them." With displeasure, the Colonel snatched the brilliant shackles from the General's hand and rudely dropped them on the desk. He continued talking about the possibility of eliminating the maquis if his superior could provide him with the necessary number of soldiers. As if not aware of what he was saying, General Auerbach extended a small white wand towards one side of the head of Colonel Harteck and a white dove appeared on his shoulder fluttering its wings. Convinced that the General was not paying attention to him in such a critical moment, the Colonel scared away the pigeon and slammed the desk with his fist, making an inkwell tremble. A small green vase spilled water. "I am speaking about serious things!" he exclaimed. Frightened with such a histrionic demonstration and such an excellent art of persuasive speech, General Auerbach dried the surface of his desk with a handkerchief and granted him the control of an entire division so he could continue with his search and destroy mission.

The plan of the Colonel consisted in surrounding Nantua, looking throughout the whole forest and closing the circle until all the maquis of the region were trapped. No one would get out of town or walk outside the boundaries of their parishes. Nobody would stroll through the streets at night or ride their bicycles. There would be no trains, telephones or telegraph services. However, the maquis had already destroyed all the railroad tracks and there were no trains in Oyonnax. Besides, they had already cut all the telephone lines, coiled them and concealed them in their houses. There were very few who rode bicycles and nobody walked at night.

One morning, two *Wehrmacht* soldiers, driving a truck armed with a tripod-mounted MG34 machine gun, ran across a French woman who was carrying a bicycle over her shoulders. The vehicle stopped suddenly, raising dust and making its brakes creak. Looking mercilessly at the French villager one of the soldiers asked her with a threatening voice:

"Don't you know that it is forbidden to use bicycles?"

There was a tense moment. Nobody spoke. The only noise was that of the vehicle's engine. The soldier, who was in charge, swung the machine gun and aimed it at the French woman. He was going to shoot when she accommodated the bicycle on her shoulders and said:

"*Monsieur*, this bicycle is broken. Neither the brakes nor the shocks work. For this reason, I am carrying it on my shoulders. I am taking it to the repair shop. I am not using the bicycle, *monsieur*... Instead, the bicycle is using me."

The two Nazis remained perplexed and looked at each other. The one asking the questions said to the driver:

"She's right. Isn't she?"

"*Ja, ja, ja,*" (Yes, yes, yes) said the other. "She's right."

"So then, let's go... *Wir haben's eilig!*" (We are in a hurry!)

They continued on their trip. The French woman carried her bicycle for a few more moments. When she was sure that the Nazis were far away and they would not return, she lowered the bicycle to the ground and made it bounce a few times. Then, she mounted the bicycle and continued her journey.

7

JEAN-YVES

"I will tell you how he interrogated me, *monsieur*. His men tortured me just like the others. They beat me until my face was unrecognizable. They burned my whole body with cigarette butts. Here, there, further down. One day he ordered his assistants to hold me standing still in the center of the room. While Goulé Tourdé held my arms, the lieutenant put the tip of a huge nail on top of my foot. With a hammer, he fastened it to the floor. Blood sprang out quickly and dripped down the sides forming a small puddle around my foot. The pain was intolerable and although I was screaming loudly, he did not hesitate to do the same with my other foot. I remained nailed down to the floor, *monsieur*. It was impossible to move. I howled from pain, looking at them, while they laughed at me. It was impossible to raise my feet because the pain was unbearable. Giggling he asked me: "Where are you going, *kamerade?*" I continued wailing. He threatened to leave me in that position until I decided to tell him the name of the maquis, who had blown up the locomotive of a train departing for Auschwitz. They left the place still laughing and celebrating as if they had told the greatest joke of their lives. I remained naked in this position for several days. When I started to fall asleep, my body would lean to one side and would revive the pain. Three days later, they removed the nails; but I could not walk for a month. After that, the wounds became infected and they took a long time to heal. The shackles left marks on my wrists. My chest and my belly were full of painful burns left by the electroshocks. They tried everything on me. They submerged me in a tub of frozen water and later they made me run over a footpath full of burning stones. The worst happened at the beginning, *monsieur*, when I arrived to that prison. Up to these days, I have terrible nightmares. He ordered his dog to attack me. Before that, he played a record with a Munich Speech on the phonograph. Hitler's voice, rough and angry, resounded very clearly through the loudspeakers. *"Das ist nicht notwendig zuzunehmen ... das Prestige der nationalen sozialistischen Bewegung... Deutschland braucht mehr Raum..."* There he stopped. There was a long and thunderous applause. A moment of silence followed and he spoke again... *"Pazifismus ist die maximale Feigheit..."* There were murmurs and laughter. I heard the long applauses... The Doberman was black, huge and wild. He had pointed ears and an iron collar with spikes around his neck. He barked angrily at me. Afterwards he ordered the dog to attack. It was a ferocious beast. He violently jumped at me snarling, while showing his white fangs. His growling made me shiver. Every time he jumped on me, it seemed that he was going to bite something off. I did everything possible to keep him away. It was horrible, *monsieur*. I thought he was going to devour me alive. Growling, the animal bit my clothes and easily tore them off. Next, he sank his teeth into my chest and shaking his head removed a portion of my flesh and swallowed it. The pain was intolerable. It was incredible, *monsieur*. He was eating me alive. The lieutenant incited him to bite me more: "To his throat, Wolf! To his throat! Higher!" Then he redirected his attention to Hitler's speech... *"Ich glaube dass als ein Nationaler Sozialist... I appear before the eyes of many bourgeois democrats as a savage. But as such, I still believe that I am a better*

European than them..." There was more applause. The dog continued rushing towards me. I leaned backwards, covered my head and tried to keep him away with my elbows. The lieutenant changed his tactic. He ordered the Doberman to bite me below the belt. The animal rushed towards my genitals and roaring wildly he ripped open my pants with one single bite. I felt his teeth graze my skin and I believe I escaped by a few millimeters. I developed an enormous fear, *monsieur*. I went into a panic attack and howled without stopping. Howl and howl. He kept inciting him: "Lower, Wolf! That's right! Lower, Wolf, lower!" I thought the animal was going to emasculate me and swallow everything he could tear off. He stopped the dog. I continued crying possessed by an intense fear. He calmed the Doberman and petted his neck. The animal remained seated near his feet, moaning, looking anxiously, licking his lips and panting. The speech ended. Again, with my whole body shaking out of pure fright and my eyes coming out from their orbits because of the sheer horror, I heard long and thunderous applauses. It seemed that the cheers were not going to end. I didn't know if the clapping was for Hitler's speech, or for the lieutenant, for torturing me in such a vicious way. Obviously it was not for me, *monsieur*; it was not for me..."

8

THE MARSEILLAISE

The death of a prisoner during an interrogation was something terrible because a valuable source of information was being lost, perhaps the one that the interrogator had wanted for a long time. On the other hand, for the prisoners it was something very moving because one of their comrades had resisted to the end without giving away any information. When that happened, they sang the *Marseillaise*. They slowly stood up, gazed at the victim who had just expired and sang without caring about the lieutenant. One of those occasions occurred when Antoinette died. Their spirits caught fire immediately. At the moment her soul was leaving, they carried the tune of the *Marseillaise*.

"*Allons enfants de la patrie...*"

It was like a farewell, like a tribute to her sacrifice.

"*Le jour de gloire est arrivé!*"

Klaus became mad and ordered them to remain silent.

"Shut up! *Wo der Führer ist, ist der Sieg!*" (Where the Führer is, there is victory!)

He slapped a prisoner; but he kept on singing.

"*L'entendard sanglant est levé...*"

"*Halt die Schnause!* (Shut your mouth!)"

He struck another prisoner; but she, courageously, continued singing.

"*Entendez vous dans les campagnes...*"

They would not stop. Instead, they sang in a booming voice, with more strength and more emotion.

With his face flushed with embarrassment, he went from one side of the room to the other, stopping in front of each one of the inmates, scrutinizing their eyes, insulting them; but they continue singing. Then he pulled out his pistol and with a ferocious gesture aimed it at their heads. It seemed that he was going insane.

He put the tip of his gun on the forehead of one of the prisoners and pressed hard.

"Mugir ces féroces soldats?"

The detainee stared at him straight in the eyes with a mocking gesture.

"Ils viennent jusque dans nos bras..."

He thought he was already dead; but he kept on singing. They had decided to intone the *Marseillaise* even at the risk of perishing.

Klaus did not shoot. He could not pull the trigger.

"Aux armes, citoyens..."

Finally, he guessed the intention of the captives and decided to do the opposite. He calmed down and smiled. Then he laughed with sarcasm and returned the pistol to its holster.

"Formez vos bataillons..."

He ordered his guards to take them back to their cells.

"Marchons Marchons..."

The soldiers prodded them with their machine guns and the inmates marched through the corridors singing. The prisoners who were in their cells joined in the song. The entire prison of Montluc rattled with the sounds of the *Marseillaise*. It is possible that everybody heard them all throughout the city of Lyon, including the Place Bellecour and the bridges.

The warbling continued for a long time. They remembered Antoinette and sang again the first couplet and the refrain. They continued until it became dark and they fell asleep out of plain weariness. There was a last throat clearing and everything remained in silence.

Meanwhile Klaus had gone out to the *Lapin Blanc* restaurant, to have dinner with Odette. He enjoyed the specials of the day, *Jambon persille, Oeufs in meurette* and *Saumon aigrelette*. That was his style, shifting very smoothly from a very traumatic experience to a pleasant one. However, the Frenchmen cheated him and that was enough for them.

9

THE VISITORS

One morning a flock of parrots flew over the Saône River and arrived at the building of the *E'Cole de Santé Militaire,* where Klaus was conducting an interrogation. The birds landed on the telephone wires and the electrical posts. Then, they flew to the window of Klaus's office and advanced slowly grabbing the edges with their claws and their yellow curved beaks. They had green feathers; their heads were red. Their eyes were small and brown, surrounded by a white halo. They looked at the interior of the office talking and moving their heads.

Klaus loved birds. As soon as he saw them, he stopped the interrogation and came up to the glass to see them. The birds seemed to be speaking to him. He opened the window and the parrots flew inside in a rush, one after the other. Fluttering their wings, they landed on the desk, the bookshelves and the piano. One of them, with the help of its thick yellow beak, climbed on the bronze hat hanger. Another one grasped the frame of Hitler's portrait with his claws and walked sideways on top of it. The black *Doberman* became restless, sniffed repeatedly and moaned faintly. The dog looked at the visitors anxiously; but did not abandon his position. Smiling, the interrogator came near the parrot standing on the bronze hanger and offered his hand. The bird, with its small dark eyes and half-opened yellow beak, raised a claw and grabbed his finger. Walking sideways on it, the visitor said with a deep voice:

"*Camerade, bonjour... camerade, bonjour...*" ("Good morning, comrade...")

"*Bonjour,*" replied Klaus.

Opening its wings widely, the bird continued:

"*Je voudrais une paire de chaussures avec un espace pour mes quatre doigts.*" (I would like a pair of shoes, with space for my four toes.)

It seemed strange to him that a parrot could ask for a pair of shoes with space for its four toes.

"*Je suis à l'étroit... Avez-vous une pointure plus grande?*" (My feet hurt... Do you have a little bigger?)

Klaus laughed. Everybody laughed. Even the prisoner, with his puffy eyes, smiled.

The bird, clumsily grasping the electrical wires with its yellow beak, raised the red feathers of its head and said:

"*Dominique, Dominique... Une bouteille de vin, s'il vous plait...*" ("Dominique, Dominique... A bottle of wine, please...")

An anarchic conversation followed in which all the parrots spoke at the same time, but none seemed to understand the other.

"*Je suis constipé.*" ("I'm constipated.")

"*Excusez-moi, je ne comprends pas... Pierre? Pierre?*"

The one standing over a thick red book opened its green wings separating its feathers, stretched one leg and said:

"*Mein Kampf! Oui? Oui?*"

"*Voilá!*" exclaimed the interrogator. "This is amazing. How does it know?"

Then the parrot let some wet, gray droppings fall over the red cover of the book. Spreading its feet and looking down at it, the bird said:

"*Qui est l'auteur de ce tableau?* (Who's the author of this painting?) Breton, Breton... Is it surrealism?... I'm dreaming, Dominique..."

"*Camerade? Camerade?*," asked the one pulling the electrical wires with its yellow beak.

"Yes."

"*Camerade... A quelle heure part l'train pour Auschwitz?*" ("At what time does the train to Auschwitz leave?")

For a moment, Klaus seemed unable to understand.

The parrot asked again:

"*Oui, oui. Pour Auschwitz. Vous ne me comprenez pas? A quelle heure?*" ("Don't you understand? At what time?")

"How much is the ticket to Auschwitz?" asked the one carefully standing on top of Hitler's portrait.

Klaus became very serious.

"*Est-ce un train direct?*" ("Is it a direct train?")

He flushed and glared at them with hatred. However, the one who offended him the most was the one walking clumsily over the piano, making noise with its claws pressing on the black and white keys. *Tlan, tlon, tlin, tlan, tlon.*

"Death to Hitler!... *Abas les Boches!*" (Down with the Germans!)

"What!" Klaus said getting rid of the parrot on his finger. He opened his holster and pulled out his pistol.

"*Mort à Hitler!* (Death to Hitler!)" screamed another parrot walking sideways.

He aimed at the parrot and pulled the trigger several times, but the pistol got jammed. All the birds flew inside the room in chaos and disorder. Finally, the weapon fired and a big explosion resounded throughout the room. The bullet made a hole in the piano and smashed two keys. The parrot ducked and said, "Almost, almost!" The dog barked and jumped trying to catch one of the birds. There was the smell of gunpowder while green feathers floated around. The parrots went out through the window and flew towards the telephone lines. From the distance, one of them squawked again:

"*Mort à Hitler! Mort à Hitler!*"

Klaus fired his pistol once more; but didn't hit any of them. The flock dispersed behind the trees. A squad of soldiers on motorcycles, wearing thick goggles, passed through the street at that moment. Because of the intense noise of their engines, they did not hear anything. The lieutenant closed the window and continued the violent interrogation.

10

TOWARDS BERLIN

After the *Wehrmacht* decided to abandon the beautiful streets and plazas of Lyon, the maquis, with a list of names and addresses, searched from house to house for the collaborators, friends and sympathizers of the Nazis. They went after the women who had shamelessly danced with them during the noisy parties at the Royal Hotel. They apprehended the consenting cooks who had beaten the egg yolks with flour to prepare the best *Crêpes soufflés* for the officers and they took into custody the *garçons* who had brought to their tables the best green bottles of champagne *Crémant d'Alsace* with golden labels and the steaming big red lobsters with their claws opened.

They arrested the hotel owners who, smoking cigars, had sent to them lovely blond women with black veils, splendid bosoms and borrowed fur coats. In like manner, they brought out to the streets the attractive Nazi-lovers, with powdered cheeks, who liked to smoke from thin black cigarette holders, at the elegant tables, imitating Marlene Dietrich, drinking sparkling *champagne* from big crystal cups while grasping the hands of the German officers, in search of love and passion. They were magnificent women with dazzling faces and inciting bodies, sometimes dressed in Nazi uniform themselves, accused of horizontal collaboration with the enemy. The maquis made them sit down on stools over the cobblestone streets, even when they were pregnant, and cut their hairs to the snuff.

The Mayor of Oyonnax, on his motorcycle, smoothing his white moustache, ordered the capture of those who had helped Colonel Fritz Harteck to chase and harass the members of the Resistance. He gave orders for the arrest of the young soldiers who had executed the wine maker who was replacing the Mayor, and Mr. Delestraint, the cheese manufacturer who had come to visit him.

Likewise, the members of the Resistance brought the maidens of the *So Ein Tag*, who had danced with the adolescent German soldiers and had fallen in love with them; the tender young women, who had waited for them every morning, with the intention of playing the music they liked on the phonograph; those who remembered their childish faces, their blue eyes, their gray uniforms and the red roses that they made appear with the snap of their fingers and the clicking of their heels.

Once seized, the maquis forced these young soldiers to get rid of their helmets, belts and uniforms, and walk to the square of Oyonnax. There they painted their naked bodies white, including their private parts. Over the ivory layer, they drew large black swastikas on their backs and chests. The young soldiers cried, like sad mimes, calling for their mothers, after learning that they had become practice targets for the maquis, in the same way the Russian prisoners had become bull's-eyes for the soldiers of Marshall Field Friedrich von Paulus at the outskirts of Stalingrad.

They also brought a band to play the happy tunes of the *So Ein Tag* and forced the sobbing maidens to attend the spectacle before initiating the ceremony of the hair cutting. The Mayor, on his motorcycle, ordered the young recruits to run so the maquis could discharge their weapons. In the middle of the outcry, the shots and the exaltation of the people, he offered a bottle of the best

Côtes du Rhône to the one who could hit the center of a swastika.

Already, by the winter of 1944, the members of the *Wehrmacht* understood that their situation in Lyon was a desperate one. They feared that they were losing the war. The Tiger II tanks did not patrol the streets aiming at the Cathedrals, at the public buildings or at the people, anymore. The officers became suspicious and spoke softly in restaurants and bars. They did not dare to sing the *Horst Wessel* in public or to display their beautiful lovers with fur coats any longer. No one attended the public spectacles. There were no dances or parties. They removed the huge portraits of Hitler from the walls of their offices and hid them in secret places. They also became convinced that the Aryan superiority was only a myth invented by Hitler so that the German Army could support his dreams of conquest and *his delirium of grandeur*. If the Germans were a superior race, the Nazi predominance, so proudly proclaimed in all directions, would not be crumbling.

Colonel Harteck suffered the most, because during those cold nights he began having nightmares in which he saw a Roman emperor wearing a white gown and a red robe. Emerging from a vanishing fog, the terrifying spirit spoke to him with a heavy Italian accent and a resounding voice:

"Leave this town right now, vicious *Germani* dog. Otherwise, my guards will slice you up and throw your mangled body to the lions... This is Lugdunum, my city. I am Claudius, *L'imperatore di Roma!"*

The following night he had another terrifying vision. A different Roman emperor, more robust and older, emerged from the darkness with his white and golden garment. He came close to Colonel Harteck, stared at him with resented eyes and showed him the dry blood he had on his face, neck and chest. He asked the Colonel:

"Hey, hey, look at this! Touch it. Don't be afraid. *Non abbia paura. Tocchi il mio sangue qui, sulla mia faccia.* Touch my face. Touch it!"

Harteck did not dare to move and hid his hand behind his back. Then slowly the emperor said with a loud and hoarse voice:

"Get out of this city, drunken barbarian! My horses and I conquered these lands. We galloped over them with pride. Therefore, they belong to me. No one else can occupy it. Go back to your trees, behind the Rhine and *pipì lì, spruzzi sopra i vostri grilli...* You belong there, not here. Look at yourself. You are afraid of me now! I can see it in your eyes. You fear me. We conquered you before. We can conquer you now. So, get out of Lugdunum!"

Then, the infuriated specter turned around and briskly walked away towards the darkness. He passed by the side of a marble statue and looking at it he said with a more calmed voice:

"*Capezzolo di Venus...* (Nipples of Venus.) I kiss you."

The next day, Colonel Harteck spoke to General Auerbach about his nightmares. The elderly officer patiently listened to what he said, while examining carefully an ancient and rusty shackle used to incarcerate gladiators, deceivers and tax evaders, during the times of Emperor Nero. When the melodious *Prelude of Lohengrin* was heard on the radio, the senior General passed his hand through his white silvery hair and unbuttoned the collar of his *S.S.* uniform. Then he lifted his cup of *cognac* from the table and said:

"Although it is true that all our successes and failures are ruled by the Nazi Party and by the Zodiac signs at the moment of our birth, my dear *kamerade,* I believe that your transits must be entangled, almost to the point of being chaotic. Because you are showing a very strange mixture of madness and idiocy, which might not be healed by anything except by the intervention of Saturn. Speaking in plain German, as Schopenhauer used to say, what else would those silly visions mean?... Emperors... Blood... Ghosts... Demons... Spirits... I regret not having a magic trick to make your lunatic dreams disappear, *kamerade,* as if they were doves or wristwatches. However, it is obvious that in your efforts to demonstrate your loyalty to the Great Third Reich, you have lost your wits and now you belong to a house for the insane. In this case, why don't you visit *Madame Josephine*? In her youth, she used to be an astonishingly gorgeous and respectable whore. So beautiful and so gentle. You could fall in love with her. For this reason, she charged double for her services and people paid gladly for it. Besides that, she possessed a sweet tongue and an astonishing talent for telling heart breaking tales and saying splendid comments. Now, retired, she dedicates herself to the fortune telling of her former clients. She is a Zodiac expert. By the way, you should know that our *Führer* is a firm believer in the influence of the planets on our actions. Besides, *Madame Josephine* is very good in healing certain ailments. Among the maladies in which she insists being better than Nostradamus and Galenus, the genius of Pergamon, is the diabolical insomnia. Of course, *kamerade,* as it should be expected, some of her clients have become deaf and dumb permanently or have ascended silently to heavens, with their shivering souls raising an arm and exclaiming *Heil, Hitler!,* after drinking her beverages in a dose higher than the indicated one. In general terms, I could assure you that the little dark syrup, she prepares with ancient plants and roots from her own garden in Lyon while reciting prayers that come directly from the Temple of Venus in ancient Rome, will perform miracles for you. That dark and foul-smelling potion will help you recover from the apparition of those bleeding phantoms that torment you at night and will restore your wits, Colonel, I am sure of it. Why don't you see her? She has even been consulted by our *Führer*…"

The following weeks the nightmares became more clear and defined. The bogeyman would come so close to Colonel Harteck that he could clearly see the wrinkles on Emperor Claudius' greasy and unshaven face, the moles on his cheeks and the short gray hairs poking out of his nostrils. The smell of wine was very strongly felt. He also observed his dusty wreath and his drooping eyes full of hatred. The Colonel noticed that the emperor, as pale as a marble statue, stumbled while walking. The image then spoke to him in a hoarse and rude voice:

"Don't talk to me about women, barbarian *Teutoni*. They are my weakness and my delight. Where is Messalina? Why isn't Messalina here for dinner and love? Call Messalina! Bring her here even if she is making love! Look for her in her bedroom and deliver her here as you find her. She must be enjoying the pleasures of passion with one of the guards. I turn around, I trip a little, I hobble, and she is already, behind my back, making love with someone else. She loves when other men forcefully penetrate her deeply from all sides, until she screams of pain and pleasure, but she doesn't allow me to do the same. I should throw her to the lions and see her body mangled and eaten by those beasts. But, what despairing guilt will erode my soul afterwards? Ah, how unsolvable my tragedy is... The mushroom, *Suevi*, the mushroom! Hey! Pay attention to what I am saying. There are no tricks here. Listen! Beware of the mushrooms. Avoid them! Smell them, but don't eat them. *Evitare di loro!* Agrippina gave me one. She dipped it in olive oil and asked me to bite a little piece. I did. That's why I am here... You have to abandon Lugdunum, *Suevi*. Leave tonight with your useless soldiers. I am telling you. This is no place for you... If you stay longer, by Jupiter!, I swear that you will end up in the lion's stomach and will come out covered by its bloody stools."

At that moment, Colonel Harteck awoke extremely terrified. Screaming, he sat up on his bed with his blond hair falling over his forehead covered by perspiration. When his alarmed *aid de camps* entered the room, they could not wake him up. They slapped his back and chest. One of them climbed to the bed and smacked his cheek, the hardest he could. However, the Colonel could not be aroused. With his wide-opened blue eyes and his sweat-covered forehead he kept staring with horror at his empty hand, rubbing it continuously and saying:

"The lion's blood! Clean its blood from my hands! Clean my legs and my butt. I am soiled. The lion passed me through his guts!"

He sloppily rubbed his hands, possessed by an intense terror. It was difficult for him to wake up completely, so he suffered the utter fear for a few more moments. However, he slowly recovered. After seeing his big white pillows and the black trunk at the foot of his bed and after hearing the sonorous tick-tock of his Victorian alarm clock over his night desk he realized that he was completely safe in one of the rooms of the Terminus Hotel, with a magnificent view of the Place Bellecour, surrounded by his smiling *aid de camps* who tried to make him understand that his hands were actually clean. Progressively, the Colonel convinced himself that he had become a victim of witchery. He probably had been given a magic elixir contained in a bottle of wine, brought by a spectacular *brunette*, who had flirted with him during one of the celebrations at the Royal Hotel.

A few days later, the Royal Air Force attacked Lyon. Seven hundred B17 and B24 bombers flew over the city, one after the other, dropping deadly explosives and leaving enormous craters everywhere. They destroyed the *E'cole de Santé*. The roofs and walls collapsed trapping the Gestapo officers who were torturing innocent prisoners at that moment.

Klaus escaped because of his good fortune. The passage of the airplanes dropping shells dazzled him. He never imagined that something like that could be possible, not even if Hitler in person could have commanded them. He emerged unharmed from the ruined bathroom, with his whole body covered in dust. He arose from the debris without trousers, stunned by the impact of the explosions, shaking off the dusty black Gestapo jacket that had become the only recognizable piece of clothing on him. He was so shocked that he could not understand what had happened or what he was doing there. He did not even realize that he could not hear. He got up and sat down several times like a mime, with a face covered by dust, rubbing his hands when there was no need to do that. It took him half an hour to realize that he had escaped alive.

Now that you are stunned, amazed, naked, and covered by ashes, evil monster, don't you remember that you sent the children of Izieu to a concentration camp where a malignant ogre with only one eye, was waiting for them? How could you, lover of Odette, and assassin of your own men and your own child, arrest three-year-old kids who despite their age understood that they had to walk with their hands up? Weren't they, while being watched by a giant monster in Nazi uniform, the ones who intoned children songs and played in the patios of the Auschwitz concentration camp before they entered the gas chambers bringing with them their plush little bears? Can't you listen to them saying, "What is that, mommy?" They were the children of Izieu, diabolical monster. Don't you remember? Didn't they eat Tarte aux pommes also? Then, I think I am going to throw you to the lions... I am Otto, emperor of Berlin...

The morale of the Resistance was raised knowing that the invasion of Normandy had been a success and that the Allied Forces were advancing through the French countryside towards Paris and Lyon. The maquis fought with more bravery because they knew that fresh armies were coming to their aid. They were not afraid of confronting their enemies on the streets and fight with the soldiers of the *Wehrmacht* anymore. They blocked the roads with fallen trees and the Germans officers had to stop their *citroens* frequently to remove the obstacles. In some towns, heralds read aloud proclamations announcing provisional governments. They shot collaborators on the squares in front of everybody or hung them from the trees, with signs attached to their chests. In that way everyone could know who they were during the shameful German occupation.

The Gestapo officers were victims of generalized terror. There was no one who could wish to exclaim: *"Vorwärts, immer vorwärts!"* That belonged to the past. There was no Panzer II tank, which could dare to point their heavy cannons at the crowds. The German officers did not believe in the Aryan superiority myth anymore. They instead acted irrationally and fired their weapons blindly against anything that would move in the streets or in the parks. Berlin gave the order to initiate a peaceful and civilized retreat. The Gestapo received instructions to carry out the Final Cleansing and Klaus burned all the telegrams confirming the transportation of prisoners by train to Auschwitz and all the evidence that could prove his participation in the capture of the children of Izieu. He destroyed the lists with the names and addresses of the women who had come to the parties at the Royal Hotel and incinerated all the reports obtained during the interrogations and the names of the officers who conducted them. He also eliminated the victims, who had survived the tortures and who could testify against him later on.

At that time, Colonel Harteck had his final nightmare. He saw Emperor Claudius approaching in a hurry, stumbling, until he was on his back, immobilizing him with a sharp dagger to his throat, saying:

"Enough is enough, *Germani* dog! Get out of my city! Now! Go back behind the river Rhine or I will set you on fire until you burn like a piece of *merda*. Or I'll throw you to the lions so you will see how they eat you alive. You will see their fangs getting deep into your flesh and you will feel a terrible pain. For the last time, get out of Lugdunum!"

At that moment, Emperor Claudius slashed his throat and Colonel Harteck fell down unconscious; but he woke up immediately and jumped up to his feet, terrified, rubbing and examining his throat to confirm that he did not have any mortal wounds.

Perspiring profusely, Colonel Harteck decided to abandon his elegant room and rapidly put his black uniform on and buttoned his jacket unequally. He left the chamber putting his boots on, called his *aides de camp* and ordered all his men to gather at the entrance of the Terminus Hotel at that moment. He had enough with lion gullets and burning stakes. Once he left through the main door, he observed the ogival windows of the elegant hotel and the tall fence that surrounds it. In that moment he noticed that he had the wrong boot on the wrong foot. They marched towards the square; but he stood still for a moment in front of the bronze statue of Louis XIV to change his boots and said to himself. "No one can eliminate the French Resistance. The Cesars of Rome protect it." Then he and his men, in a hurry, finished crossing the Place Bellecour searching for the Rhône's bridge.

The rest of the Nazi soldiers evacuated old Lugdunum after the XI Panzer Division, hurriedly in retreat, passed through the streets, fearing that the Royal Air Force with their seven hundred B17 and B24 bombers would hit them again. They spent all their time looking at the skies, afraid that the airships will suddenly appear gliding over their heads. The legendary Panzer II tanks, with 75 millimeters cannons and two machine guns, advanced at full speed without allowing their engines to stop for any reason and passed over the bridges of the Rhône and the Saône. Behind them, the undefeatable and proud soldiers of the *Wehrmacht* advanced quickly towards Berlin, already without canteens, rifles or daggers.

The commander of the Montluc prison surrendered the building to the members of the Resistance. He gave a brief speech emphasizing on the fallacy of the Aryan superiority over any other race of the world; but gave a Nazi salute. He returned a hoop of keys, turned around and ran desperately through the streets of Lyon, looking backwards, fearful that the laughing maquis would decide at any time to shoot him on the back.

Klaus evacuated the city after destroying the incriminating documents he kept at the Terminus Hotel. He burned thousands of letters, memorandums and telegrams. The only thing he regretted was to abandon the huge oil portrait of Hitler he still kept in his office and the black records with round yellow labels, containing the *Führer's* speeches. He went around the city looking for his former collaborators who had attended him during his torture sessions and witnessed the times he had shot his victims on the back of their heads. After finding them, even when his assistants were greeting him in a very amiable fashion, he coldly murdered them without giving any explanation.

Meanwhile, the legendary and invincible soldiers of the *Wehrmacht*, unquestionable conquerors of Warsaw, Paris and Amsterdam, were fleeing in disorder, cursing Goebbels and Göring for convincing them that God had sent the *Führer* and his generals to save Germany. Instead, they had led them to the most humiliating and shameful defeat. The Mayor of Oyonnax and his maquis, chased them through roads and open fields. When they found them, he asked. "Who belongs to a superior race, now?" He shot at the ground with his revolver so the soldiers would run faster. "*Stürm* the roads now, so you will *stürm* Berlin tomorrow," he told them. At the outskirts of Lyon some prostitutes threw stones at them screaming: *"A Bas les Boches!"* One of the women grabbed a branch and lashed the bottom of one of the young Nazi soldiers, who decided to run quicker. "If the sluts were insulting and shaming them, what will history think of them?" they thought. The German soldiers tore off their swastikas, threw them violently to the ground and ran because they could hear that the allied bombing of the seven hundred B17 and B24 bombers was getting louder and louder. In the towns the soldiers only found dead animals, tilted wagons and fallen comrades.

General Auerbach retreated towards Berlin, advancing slowly on a mule, despite the nearby explosions. He was followed by two soldiers who were carrying his trunks, with removable hinges and iron locks, in which he kept his costumes, sabers, hats and shackles used during his magic acts. Quietly, the General was rehearsing with a mouse and a piece of cheese in order to refine a new magic trick.

Limping, Klaus escaped with a gunshot wound to the foot. After a long journey, on trains and carts, he arrived to the Black Forest and requested admission to Saint Peter Hospital. The medical care and the food were superb. However, whenever he remembered Odette, he had bouts of intense fright. Once, while they were cleaning his infected wound with cotton balls dipped in iodine, he recalled the day he went with Odette to have lunch at the *Lepin Blanc*. At that moment, insidiously, a panic attack grew within his chest. The terror became so intense that he stood up, pushing away the instrument cart, he went around the ward, stumbling against chamber pots and beds. He screamed and pulled his hair, stretched his mouth with his fingers and violently poked his eyes with whatever he found at hand. He banged his head against the wall repeatedly, howling like a mad man. The medical personnel put a straight jacket on him for several days. After he recovered from this acute crisis, with injections of camphor and cups of Valerian infusions, he remained in complete silence, without making any movements, for about a month. Afterwards, they transferred him to a Halberstadt sanatorium for convalescents.

At the last moment, due to his nagging requests, his superior officers promoted him to the rank of *Sicherheitzdienzt* Captain. They awarded this ranking because of his attempts to destroy the French Resistance during the war and because of the heinous crimes he committed against innocent civilians in the name of Adolf Hitler and the glorious Third Reich. Nevertheless, his commanding officers advised him to disappear from Germany immediately.

11

TOTENTANZ

I am Otto, emperor of Berlin. I am here to tell you all about this blazing night. So, look attentively at the scales of my fish. Observe the little, shiny scales of my flounder. Yes, a flounder. Look at them. Tiny, gray, black, bright... This morning, this flounder was swimming at the bottom of the Baltic Sea. *Now it hangs from my neck...* Someone makes noise in the adjacent room. Whispers, laughs and moans. Banging sounds on an old bed, rhythmic, energetic and anxious. German lips over German lips, pressing hard against each other. *Nibelungen. Lippenstift.* Brother and sister satisfy each other with great lover's passion. There is a strong smell of beer. *I love Deibels... My favorite... That wonderful bitter taste...* Before going inside, the lieutenant left his jacket on the dining room chair. The black jacket had the image of a golden eagle on its pocket. On the *telefunken,* a happy melody of Wagner: *The Dance of the Prentices* of *Die Meistersinger von Nürnberg.* It is part of the nighttime program of Radio Berlin. Soon a persistent buzzing intensifies; the cups and the glazed earthenware, with their blue designs, tremble on the wooden ledge, below the framed black and white photograph of the *Führer.* At first, they shudder delicately; then, uncontrollably. A vase falls down and smashes on the floor. Immediately, there is a sharp whistling sound, followed by a thunderous, majestic explosion, which intensely illuminates the entire room. The windows explode into small pieces of glass falling everywhere. The room remains lit up by a great brightness. After a few seconds, Gerda finds that all she can hear is the soft and happy clanking of the small bells of *Die Meistersinger,* which go *in crescendo,* producing a clear and exquisite melody. There is a strong smell of smoke. Her braided blond hair, as that of Rapunzel, has small glass fragments glittering in the darkness. The portrait of Hitler, on fire, has fallen over a heap of small particles of broken crystals. Another explosion rattles the apartment, illuminating it. Gerda falls down and bangs her head against the table. She feels cold and all the hairs of her body rise at the same time. She wants to cry, but restrains herself. The screams and exclamations of the people running on *Oberwallstrasse,* trying to escape from the string of incendiary explosions, are very clearly heard as well as the howls and barking of the dogs. There is a dense black smoke in the room. Hastily, the two naked lovers evacuate the chamber and run between the furniture and the moving tongues of fire. Yellow flames undulate and climb over the walls. A bad smell becomes intolerable and makes it almost impossible to breathe. Gerda perceives the intense heat of the creaking flames coming closer, burning her face.

Other Berliners emerge from their dwellings and look at the Lancaster bombers of the Royal Air Force, with their long wingspan and their four helixes, rumbling over their roofs, dropping high explosives and incendiary bombs. The gunfire of the German artillery appears in the darkness as well as the searching lights crossing the sky in all directions. The explosions are unending. Berliners are horrified and cannot think properly or concentrate on what they are doing. It is the fear of the *Totentanz* flying over the big city. *Where is Hitler with all his microphones and vehement speeches? Where is the one who said, in a speech addressed to the Nazi Youth, that the young Germans were the blood of their blood and that Germany was following him to fulfill its destiny? Did he ever augur that one day Berliners would have to run to avoid being sucked up into a huge lake of fire? Where is Goebbels with his tight uniform and his ingenious propaganda? Maybe he doesn't want to face the public because Lida Baarova didn't want to make love to him last night. Where is Göring, the Sigfrit of the Luftwaffe, the overweight warrior of the shining golden armor who slew dragons and bathed in their blood to become immortal? Why can't he climb into his biplane and courageously clean the Germanic sky from such dreadful enemies? Tell him to come and show us why he has all those medals on his chest. Let him explain this outrageous attack on Berlin. Now from the great city only remain fragments of burned bricks and concrete blocks instead of its former marvelous futuristic buildings. Is that the fulfilled promise of the thousand years of pure Aryan blood domination by the Third Reich? Nobody warned us that the Allied Forces were capable of attacking us in this hideous way. What was our Führer thinking during his celebrated Danzig speech? Wasn't he able to envision that one day all the inferior races of the world, commanded by the dwarf Alberich, would burn us all in a hellish mass of fire? This is the revenge of Claudius, emperor of Rome, and the repayment of Nero, who would not have rested until seeing Berlin on fire, until seeing us destroyed.* People rush towards the air-raid shelters because they are afraid of being burnt alive. All Berliners are frightened with this Dance of Death, with this *Totentanz*. However, the kids of the *Deutsche Jugend* continue offering cyanide capsules; but no one is interested in them. *Has anyone taught these grandchildren of Kriemhild the secret of making a good fire for the incinerators at a concentration camp? What is the best way to exterminate one hundred prisoners, in the shortest lapse of time? It is to burn a lot of coal and timber with the cold-hearted spirit of a German dragon. Also needed are a great passion for the motherland and a Nazi obsession.* Berliners observe the Lancaster bombers of the Royal Air Force, the fuselage and the cockpit of the airplanes releasing 12,000 pounds explosives. They see the strings of incendiary bombs falling over them and hear the long whistles and the explosions. It seems that the airplanes are never going to stop bombarding the city. On the street, among burning automobiles, charred carts and people running with their children, a benevolent brown donkey lies quietly, with his old flute attached to his back. A German shepherd, sitting down by its side, with an Italian mandolin close to its foot, tries to wake him up, licking his long and hairy ears. Their companion, a green and red rooster, stands on a big drum, nervously opening his wings and singing loudly. Suddenly the jackass rises, shakes his body and brays repeatedly and sadly. All his friends rejoice. *Because if the donkey dies, how could the musicians of Bremen climb on top of each other to see through the window what the Nazi robbers are doing at the feasting table, among Rembrandts and silvery menorahs.* The shelter is full. Inside, in the darkness, women and men squat, wail and pray in a low voice. They perceive the smell of a good lager, but are unable to think properly. They fear that, unexpectedly, the big flames thrown by the gullets of an evil dragon will get inside the shelter, engulf everyone and make them disappear. They anxiously pray so this will not occur. *Where is Knight Dietrich, the only hero who could come to defend us? Where is your golden hair, adored Rapunzel? Throw me your fair-haired plaits, dear maiden, and I'll climb the walls of your windowless castle, to love you as nobody has done it yet and to penetrate you, with great love, endlessly. I am your prince, dear Rapunzel, your beloved monarch, your crowned blind lover. I will give you as a present the mandolin of the Musicians of Bremen.*

Otto enters the refuge carrying a big banner with a colorful replica of the *Dance of Death of Lübeck.* Despite the darkness, several dancing images, holding hands, appear on the banner. One of them is the shadowy image of a Cardinal with red hat and sandals, embracing the image of Death. Another is an Empress with a silky gown and a headdress with golden ornaments. The other is Death itself, wrapped in a white shroud, holding a large torch and hugging Hitler. The *Führer* comes into view shyly smiling, wearing a white uniform with a thin belt across his chest, and raising a foot trying to take a dance step. Next to them, the image of Eva Braun, with her blond hair and her simple short sleeve dress. Otto leaves the banner leaning against the wall and uncovers his head. His white shroud, long and dirty, has a black *hackenkreus* painted on his back. Held by leather strings, a big grayish black flounder, shiny, fresh and slippery, hangs from his neck. On one of the fish's sides, there is the silhouette of a swastika made by swift knife cuts. There is an intense smell of Diebels. It comes from an enormous glass full of clear amber beer, with small bubbles rising slowly from the bottom to the head of overflowing white foam. With a stentorian voice, the actor speaks to the terrified crowd. *Listen to me, Berliners. Look at me. I am Otto, Emperor of Berlin, direct descendant of the line of Queen Ute. I am also Death. If you have never seen Death, look at me. I am She. Look now at the bright scales of my fish. Grilled flounder? Didn't you, Berliners, want to learn the thrills of being possessed by fear and horror? This is the perfect place. When you see me, don't you feel a knot in your throat that tightens and doesn't allow you to breathe? This is it. Don't waste your time watching burned enchanted castles from the kingdom of the Amelungs. Drink this beer instead and join me in my Dance. Sip and verify that all of us can turn into the same rottenness after being killed by these bombs. Tomorrow, once the bombarding has ended, the raping will begin. Before sunrise the soldiers of the Russian Army, the ones who defeated us in Stalingrad and the Vistula, those who have shamefully chased us to this wonderful city of Berlin, will be in the streets, smelling of vodka, aiming their machine guns at us, looking for our women.*

The dark gray flounder hanging from his neck is fresh and has two yellow eyes on one side of its flat head, close to the open mouth. *Herr Führer, where are you? Please drop your cap and join my Dance. Come and try this broiled fish I have prepared... Vegetarian? Was ist das Tagesgericht?... Flunder!... Thinking, mein Führer, of a cold beer in a riesengrossem Glase? Such a bitter and wonderful flavor... Although you will commit suicide and take your delight in chewing a cyanide capsule, you will only be accelerating Death's commands. Come and hold my hand, mein Führer... Bring Eva Braun, our Queen Ute, the supreme example of the Aryan race. Come, your Majesty, beloved Führer. You are our savior. Show us your shining black boots. Move those feet, rapidly, lightly. Please, flutter around with this Totentanz. Raise the golden crucifix that I have rescued from a monastery on fire and press the tip of this Pistolen P38 against your temple. Then, pull its trigger. Tomorrow the raping of the Aryan women will start early. We the German men will be on the run. What will happen to the beautiful hairy pubis of Venus, mein Führer? What will happen to the purity of our blood? Don't you know that the rush of the heated air in the atmosphere can create a vacuum that could suck the fire through all the streets flinging all human bodies into an enormous lake of fire? Did you envision this before invading Poland, before trying to take over Luxemburg? Oh, so horrible!* Inside the shelter, the smoke becomes denser. The scent of *Diebels* is stronger. *Ah, delicious Diebels... Who is drinking beer here? Are the children of the Deustche Jugend distributing them? They should apportion it among us right away. Kamerade, pass the beer, please. We want to enjoy its bitter flavor, so delicious... Come Goebbels. Drink this beer and take this glass capsule. Bite it hard. You have to extract its bitter poison and swallow it, smacking your lips. You will like it. You, the one with the small body in the tight uniform, the funny one. Didn't you make a movie of Hänsel and Gretel, the fair-haired children of the Rhineland, dressed with the Hitlerian Youth uniform, both of them drunk, holding big glasses of beer? Didn't they travel mounted on the back of a swan, flying over the surface of a lake and a forest of hazelnuts, on their way to their father's hut, to announce that the Third Reich had arrived at its most glorious moment? Oh, it is so horrible to know... You, minister of propaganda, that spent your time with actresses, lifting their skirts and lowering their underwear, grabbing their buttocks and fornicating with them in your office on top of tons of papers and memorandums sent by our Führer announcing the details of the Barbarosa campaign. Tell me if you can bribe Death. Come, Goebbels, the golden era of our Greater German Reich and the era of the great speeches are over. Please, join us and remember that the most vigorous, the most robust, is the one who gets rotten faster, the one most beloved by the worms of the German cemeteries. And, your gracious wife, Magda Goebbels? The Teutonic Medea, who poisoned her children because she loved them too much. Wasn't she waiting for a very smart playwright to write her tragedy? Soon the rapes will begin in the entire city of Berlin. They will occur in the open air. Behind the smoke and over the burnt ruins, among the explosions, while the survivors will be eating the last bratwursts left in the city. Passions will be satisfied over piles of earth recently dug out and among the whistle of the bullets. It is foreseen and calculated already. Argumentum ad baculum. The moment will arrive when the soldiers of the Soviet Weltanschhauung, the Red Army, all excited, will leave their barracks, drunk with happiness, searching for the legendary Berlin women. In what position would you like to be raped, Liebe Frauen? Beautiful German buttocks... Irresistible, tender, marvelous. The most eye-filling women that ever lived in this land since the times of Queen Grunhild. Please, be original. Don't worry about racial purity. Simply, think of a position that could stun the enemy, and leave them speechless, without breath. Get down on your knees, Liebe Frauen. Bend down and touch the bed with your breasts very gently. Maintain a gesture of saintliness and innocence. Show your nylon stockings embroidered with numerous, small black swastikas, fastened with a rubber tie in the middle of your thighs. Show them your pretty and magnificent vulvae shining lightly with your sweat. Moan and tremble with each hard push... "Mein Liebe, mein Liebe..." Tell them that you wish to be possessed violently, that you want them to penetrate you and destroy you inside. Tell them that you want to feel what you never felt before. You should whisper softly: "Sneller, meine Liebe, sneller..." Don't you think so? While the soldiers of the Red Army move with impetuosity, let them hear your moans loudly. Even in defeat, you have to be superior to your enemies, Liebe Frauen. Maintain your courage, your heroism... Don't forget that you descend from the wonderful and breathtaking women of the Nietherland... And you, Herr Doktor Mengele? Try some of these incendiary bombs. Lie down on the surface of the street with your S.S. uniform, calm and comfortably and let one of the incendiary bombs fall on you... Please, come and dance with us. The glass urinals will not be of any help to you now. Didn't you practice a vivisection on the flying swan of Hänsel and Gretel and found that the bird only had green excrement inside, hard stools, in the shape of a hakenkreus? Do you remember that? Hard hakenkreuses... You threw them immediately, one by one, aiming well, against a target drawn on the wooden wall of the concentration camp. Tell me, Herr Doktor. What did you do in Auschwitz? Didn't you separate the healthy from the unhealthy? What did you do to those Hungarians dwarfs when you met with them and heard their thin and childish voices? Didn't you drink beer from an enormous glass ornamented with images of a heroin from the Grimm Brothers' fairy tales? Didn't you feel like Snow White, with an S.S. cap, among the seven dwarfs? Didn't you stitch together, a couple of screaming twins, back to back, while giving them spoonfuls of ice cream, to demonstrate that Siamese brothers could not only be separated but could also be united? Excellent idea. Nazi inspiration. Genius...* Another deafening explosion occurs near the shelter. The place shakes violently like in an earthquake. There is more smoke and dust falling rapidly from the roof. Standing people collapse and drop unconscious. No one wants to die, so everybody loses their wits. *Am I crazy? Am I?* Their lips tremble with fear. *The aroma of the Brötchen is felt with more intensity. Isn't it time for breakfast? What did the Londoners do during the Blitzkriegs of Hitler? Run and hide? Blow their noses and drink hot English tea with cream for breakfast? Did you think about that, my Führer? You did the same to them. Now, our courageous soldiers are arriving from France and Belgium, sobbing, defeated, without their guns. It is so sad to see them. Unable to find their houses or their mothers, they weep and run to the shelters, but there is no place for them. No one wants them there. The explosions continue. It seems that they are never going to cease. From the raping of the following day, no one will escape. Age will not be a concern. Panic intensifies. You should prepare and make yourself more beautiful. You should apply your lippenstift, put on your best dresses and restrain from using your underwear, please. You will never know how attractive you can be when you don't wear anything inside. What delicate and fine vulvas, so wonderful and beautiful...* Outside, several people come from the corner. They are the members of a theatrical company known as *The Dance of Dunces.* Cinder and dust cover their faces and costumes. They stare at the fire and the debris as something unreal, as if the bombing and the destruction of the buildings were a product of the imagination, as if it had nothing to do with them. At that moment, a soldier, with boots and helmet, on a motorcycle wrapped in flames, passes near them. He accelerates his machine for a short distance;

65

however he falls and continues burning. Another incendiary bomb bursts nearby provoking a big fire, which quickly spreads to the adjacent buildings. The Empress, with her golden crown, raises a hand to protect herself from the falling debris. She has painted her face in white, her eyebrows and lips, in black. She spits on one finger and passes it over her eyebrow. They just have left an orgy, in which they made love, in all imaginable ways and as many times as they could. Now they are exhausted and satisfied although their expressions are grave and serious. *"Wollen Sie mehr?,"* (Do you want more?) the Queen asks the hat-maker dressed as a XIX century dandy. *"Nein!,"* (No!) he answers. *"Genug!"* (Enough!)... From a radio comes a melody. It is the *Overtura Coriolanus Opus 62* of Ludwig van Beethoven. Next, a powerful and gigantic suction passes through the streets flinging timber, animals, and cars into the immense ball of fire. The actors fly through the air until they disappear into the large orange and yellow flames... The following day, when the sunrise brings light to the city, a huge dense cloud of smoke and dust darkens Berlin. The coal, stored in the houses, has fueled the fires, which will continue blazing for days. All the streets are in ruins. There are thin columns of white grayish smoke quietly rising from the ravages and the dead bodies. The *Totentanz* has passed during the night making her presence felt. In front of the buildings, there are piles of corpses left on iron beams. *I am dying, Berlin... after so much pleasure... So many smoking bodies. The bosoms of Rapunzel, tender and inciting, small and nubile, with her little nipples standing are now immobile. Her burnt and beautiful fair-haired braid is hanging to one side. The Froschköning sits on her chest croaking occasionally. Oh, so horrible, I am sobbing... It's so dreadful, my Führergott, to know that you will not lead us anymore... But we will follow you to the end of time... Deutschland, erwache! Es ist nichts unmöglich!* (Germany, awaken! Nothing is impossible!) *The charred corpses of the*

actors of the Dance of Dunces Theatrical Company are also on the heap; some are unrecognizable. The hand of the Queen of Hearts, black as charcoal, still with a shiny ruby ring on a finger, holds a golden scepter. Over her belly lies the swan with its widespread wings, its long white neck and its yellow beak. The remains of the hat-maker with his XIX century clothing are near by. They will remain on the street until further identification and cremation are done. On the front wall of a roofless bombarded building, a door is off its hinges. There are melted iron beams nearby. Inside, a calendar is still hanging from a ruined wall. A heap of bricks with pieces of twisted iron and blocks of concrete are in the foreground... The Rondo of the Concert for violin, D major Opus 61 by Ludwig van Beethoven comes from somewhere... So now, walk with your heads up, Berliners... Hold your chins up... Follow your Führer, to the death... Touch the dust and hold your pain. The bleeding will stop soon. Death is only one more step in life. One more step. That's all... Es ist nichts unmöglich...
(Nothing is impossible…)

12

MY ONLY CRIME IS BEING A GERMAN WOMAN

Fatalism and famine fell over the city of Berlin. After the last season concert given by the Philharmonic Orchestra, with a delicious counterpoint between the organ and the strings, in *The Cuckoo and the Nightingale,* the musicians said goodbye to each other with embraces and kisses, in a theater destroyed by the Allied bombing. At the exit of the theater, the kids of the Hitlerian Youth offered them cyanide capsules from a basket as if they were chocolate candies. It was a courtesy of the Führer, an admirer. A retribution for the countless moments of pleasure they had provided him when playing Schumann and Wagner and in gratitude for the loyal Nazi salutes the conductors gave, clicking their heels and raising an arm, before initiating the concerts.

Several days later, some musicians ended their lives, victims of dismay and melancholy, after leaving their *Cremona* violins and their *Stradivarius* violoncellos with a good neighbor or with their best friends. Suicide became an indeclinable pleasure. It was preferable to commit their own immolation rather than to confront the affliction and the shame they would suffer when the soldiers of the Soviet *Weltanschhauung,* the Red Army, would occupy the city of Berlin. Moreover, suicide by cyanide was not painful; it was instead, fascinating. There could not be greater satisfaction than to take their lives for a just cause or for the honor of the motherland.

Everyone was drunk in Berlin during those days. The city was in ruins; most of the buildings were destroyed, the houses did not have electricity and the population was deeply submerged in absolute terror. It was in those circumstances that the eroticism of the young women found its highest expression and the moment of its liberation. Possessed by the desire to achieve the ecstasy of passion and to know how it felt inside, when the male organ was fulfilling its divine command, they all wanted to make love. There were women who, obsessed by this desire, visited a dentist. After sitting down on the reclined armchair, illuminated by a potent light, they slowly raised their skirts to show that they were not wearing any panties. Completely flushed, they exposed their delicate genitalia and begged the healer to touch them gently because they could not contain themselves anymore. During those days, anyone could find love and passion in the most unexpected places.

It was the expression of fatality and fear. The *U-Bahn* ran in the places where stations had not been bombed or destroyed; but Berliners were convinced that at any moment the Allies could kill them in the streets, for pleasure or without any reason, just because they were the Germans, the defeated ones. Therefore, it was better to make love as much as possible and to spend all the Marks they had in their wallets, because within the following days, with the *bolcheviques* walking through the streets of Berlin, money would have no value.

The civilian population indulged in generalized drunkenness and in the practice of love making in a boundless way. The maidens gave themselves to strangers, in the streets or parks, since they wanted to know the exaltation of procreation before dying. They mated with the beardless boys of the Hitlerian Youth who did not know how to perform and with the mature officers who knew more than was necessary. They eagerly copulated for the first time in their lives, moaning and changing positions rapidly, moving swiftly, behind the damaged buildings and the parks in ruin. The entire city transformed itself into an enormous Bruegel painting.

After learning that such a desperate search for sexual fulfillment was going on with the German women, the heroic and disciplined soldiers of General Georgy Zhukov, the ones who fought from the destroyed buildings and from the sewers of Stalingrad, accelerated their march towards Berlin. The infantry soldiers advanced, day and night, without taking any break, even wetting their pants while crossing rivers and ponds or stumbling on the muddy hills. The Soviet T-34 tanks, with their armored turrets, their 85 mm cannons and their caterpillar tracks, increased to their maximum speed, splashing dirt and advancing over the ground, sown with grains, beets and cabbages, even while their drivers were falling asleep at the steering wheels.

It was not because they wanted to capture Berlin as a birthday present for comrade Stalin or because they wanted to take possession of the three tons of uranium oxide hidden in the Kaiser Wilhelm Institute before General George Patton could put his hands on it. In reality, it was because the brave soldiers of General Vasily Chuikov wanted to meet those beautiful Berlin maidens, who were willing to make love with anyone who came near them. All they had to do was to arrive in Berlin as soon as possible. The more they thought about this the more inebriated they became and the more audaciously they drove their vehicles on their journey to the west. It was like a fixed idea, which could not disappear; but by the contrary, intensified with the passage of time and made them exert extreme efforts in order to appear in front of the fabulous German women.

The truth was the opposite; all Berlin women were frightened with the idea that an abominable crime was going to be committed against them. Everywhere the alarmed women ran from house to house talking about the execrable transgressions that would take place soon. It was only a matter of time. *"Der Ivan kommt!,"* (The Russians are coming!) was a common expression among them; but desperation and terror would not allow them to leave town or to take measures to protect themselves from the imminent danger.

Upon their arrival to Berlin, the Russian soldiers hoisted a Victory flag, made from a red tablecloth painted with a white sickle and a hammer, at the top of Hitler's Chancellery. They did not waste time with useless ceremonies. After hanging their rifles on their shoulders and saying *"Море по колено к выпитому..."* (To a drunk man the sea can only reach up to his knees*)*, they made a toast with bottles of vodka, intertwining their arms, looking fixedly at each other's eyes and drank all they could. They dropped the empty bottles and immediately they went into the streets in search of the wonderful women who were waiting for them. It was Pieter Bruegel for everybody. "It is imperative that we find them today, *tovarich,*" said an officer. "Tomorrow it will be too late." Marshall Zhukov announced the final punishment of the German Army for besieging so viciously their beloved Russian city. "Defenders of Stalingrad!," he said. "For one day, and only for one day, Berlin is yours. Do as you wish."

Inebriated and joyful, licensed to do whatever they wanted, the brave infantrymen, the ones who had witnessed the surrender of Field Marshall Friedrich von Paulus, searched through the buildings and the ruins. When they found a woman, they dragged her despite her resistance and her screams. Other soldiers carried their children in their arms. *"Where is the *Sturm Abteilung?,*"* the women asked. Others tried to escape from the buildings. "Call the *Wehrmacht!,*" they screamed. But the Russian soldiers replied: *"Come, моя любовь,* come." ("Come, my love, come.")

The men who had bravely fought defending Stalingrad and evading the German snipers bullets, in the middle of the fetid odor of the decomposing bodies under the rubble and the debris, entered the Berlin houses. They aimed their rifles at the children's head, accusing them of being members of the Hitlerian Youth. "This is Hitler!" they said. "This is a sharpshooter! Blow his head off!" The despaired mother tried to explain that the small child had nothing to do with Hitler or with the National Socialism. Finally, the mother yielded and said. "Do with me whatever you want; but leave my child alone!" Then the smiling soldiers took the resigned woman to the bedrooms saying. *"Любовь жестокая."* (Love is cruel.)

The following day, those who had sworn to fight for Russia and for the victory of the *proletariat,* came back bringing food for the children. They behaved with benevolence and demonstrated feelings of charity and compassion. They caressed their blond hair and said loving words to them. After serving the children's meals, they took the mothers to the bedrooms and made love ceaselessly. Very tragically, for the wives of the *Wehrmacht* officers there was no one to defend them. There was no soldier with a carbine Kar98k screaming: *"Ein kampf! Ein sieg!"* who could throw a stick grenade in the middle of the bedroom, next to the squeaky bed where the ravishment was taking place, or a *Führer* who could say: *"Deutschland* needs more room!" It was unfortunate that the only ones who could defend the city of Berlin were the children; but they were in the arms of the Russian soldiers. In all the bombarded streets, there were sexual assaults, several of them carried out at the same time. On that day, any woman who was found in an open field was raped.

The Russian officers could not contain their men and considered this as a natural consequence of war. A few months before, the German soldiers had done the same with the Stalingrad women. The defeated ones had to be debauched. It was necessary to dishonor the entire population, to destroy their minds and their spirits, in order to weaken them and discipline them.

The women reacted with intense anger and shame. They could not stop weeping during the day and woke up sobbing in the middle of the night. They recalled with unexpected lucidity, the faces, the voices and the bad breath of the perpetrators. They also remembered their cylindrical hats and their infantry winter coats. These scenes invaded their minds and made them hate anything that was Russian. After a while some of the victims who, at one point in the past, had acclaimed the *Führer* in the *Reichstag* and the *Sportpalatz*, said with indignation. "There is no reason to continue living. My only crime is being a German woman."

Incapable of tolerating their tragic recollections anymore, and not having any desire to continue living, some decided to end their existence. One of them was Frederika, a beautiful Berliner with an attractive body, who a few days before had been violated, in the most villainous and repugnant way, by the infantrymen of General Konev. On the night desk she left the pen and paper, which she used to write a suicide letter. Her father, a hero of the *Luftwaffe*, had died a few months earlier. A Soviet female pilot, with the deadly fire of her machine gun, made him fall from the sky while conducting a reconnaissance flight in his Messerschmitt Me-109s over the Stalingrad outskirts. Frederika put a record with the music of the *Horst Wessel* on the phonograph and raised the volume. Soon, she undressed completely and kneeled naked in front of the little table where she had placed the Luftwaffe dagger that belonged to her father. Sitting down, with her splendid buttocks over her heels, and her beautiful hair flowing over her shoulders, she slowly unsheathed the brilliant double edge dagger and dropped the metallic scabbard. While she continued listening to the march, her beautiful hands clutched the ivory handle with a spiral design. She raised the weapon and turned it against herself. Joyfully she observed that the cross guard of the knife had the shape of an eagle with its open wings, standing over a *hakenkreus*. She had the impression that she was holding a cross in her hands. With great satisfaction, she passed her blue eyes over the clean stiletto blade and observed the brilliant surface. At that instant, she thought that it would be so fascinating to stab her own body with it. Slowly, she neared the bright tip towards her stomach until she felt the pricking pressure of the metal. How wonderful she felt. When the *Horst Wessel* was at its most emotional moment, she screamed. *"Deutschland, so wie wir kämpfen!"* (Germany, this is our fight!) Then, with all her strength, she pushed the dagger into herself. She had the sensation that she could not breathe and her blue eyes widened. Next, her vision became dark and she slowly fell to the floor.

13

INTERROGATOR INTERROGATED

Once in Berlin, walking by the Alexanderplatz area, Klaus did not recognize the nightclubs and the whorehouses where he conducted raids, by orders of the *Sicherheitsdienst*, only a few years before. Demoralized *Wehrmacht* soldiers, walked through the streets, full of rubble and debris, without their red banners with swastikas, followed by noisy dwarfs and panting dogs dressed in Nazi uniforms. The *katushia* missiles of the Soviet artillery had destroyed the walls and the spiral of the *Kaiser-Wilhelm-Gedächtnis Kirche*. The *Reichstag* and the *Sportpalatz* were unrecognizable.

The Soviets organized civilian squads to clean the city in a very strict manner. Holding a list, the soldiers made all the surviving men and women sweep the streets. Those who had acclaimed the Führer during his speech in the *Congress of the German Work Front*, had to remove the concrete blocks, the fragments of bricks and the burnt wooden beams. Those who did not remove the debris did not eat.

The population was furious with Hitler, Goebbels and Göhring. They had solemnly sworn in front of microphones and wires, with emphatic gestures, that they would lead them to the greatest victory of all times; however, the reverse had occurred. They had led them to the most humiliating defeat the German nation could ever witness. The assurance of a thousand years of world domination had been a false promise. The Aryan supremacy was a falsehood used to add more realism to the *Führer's* charlatanism. Nobody was superior to anybody. By the contrary, perhaps it was possible that Germans were inferior to other races. Beaten as they were, no one could arrive to a different conclusion. Klaus searched for the former Gestapo building and after several failed attempts, he found 8 *Prinz-Albrechtstrasse* and realized that the building had been completely demolished by the Allied bombers. The corner where he used to eat *bratwursts* with *sauerkraut* from an ambulant seller had disappeared. Only piles of dirt and debris could be seen everywhere.

As other surviving officers, Klaus had to live by his wits, selling stolen wristwatches, cans of salted fish and cigarettes from the black market. He also became very efficient in finding customers for the *Puttkamerstrasse* women. When he was convincing a grammar school student that he was about to have the greatest experience of his life, two British agents identified him, arrested him and brought him, almost by force, to the British Foreign Office.

The gestures of the agent who interrogated him displayed certain indisposition; however, his manners were gentle and elegant. On the desk, there was a jumble of letters, classified documents and carbon copies. Klaus was clearly disturbed. He flushed frequently for no apparent reason. He was mad at himself for allowing the British to capture him. The incandescent filament of the light bulb hanging from the roof reminded him of his office at the Hotel Terminus where he had tortured thousands of innocent citizens. From the adjacent room came the persistent clanking of a typewriter. He remembered Odette inserting a piece of paper with a carbon copy in her stenotype before taking her underwear off in front of him at the office of Colonel Harteck. The British agent cleaned his eyeglasses with a white handkerchief and placed them over his nose. He started by reading from an old document.

"What is your name, sir?"

Klaus flushed. Then he stood up and raising an arm exclaimed:

"*Deutschland ist Hitler! Hitler, Deutschland ist!*"

"Oh, God!" the agent said. "Not again, please. Don't get jacked off. The times to do that are gone and well past. I only asked you for your name."

"Don't you know me?" replied Klaus sarcastically. "Here, in Berlin, everybody knows me as the magician of the black market who can get the best can of anchovies and the most attractive women for the best prices. Gorgeous women, I mean..."

The agent, opening his mouth with astonishment, asked:

"Was that the last order of Adolf Hitler? To get the most gorgeous women, for the best price?"

"He never gave such an order."

"But you are a soldier. You must be following orders. Don't they say that the *Führer* was a firm believer of the occult and a genius of necromancy and precognition, capable of foretelling anything? At some point he had to predict that his officers were going to have difficult times."

"Yes, of course. But he never gave such an order."

"Very well, then... Please, tell me, what is your rank?"

"I am a *Sicherheitzdienzt* Captain."

"Aren't you a lieutenant?"

"I was promoted by the end of the war. They also rewarded me with the Iron Cross."

"The Iron Cross with the red and blue ribbon?"

"Yes."

"And as a Captain of the *Sicherheitzdienzt,* with your Iron Cross around your neck, do you have to walk the streets and get clients for the prostitutes of the *Puttkamerstrasse*? An extraordinary idea! Whose idea was that? Hitler or *Obersturmbanführer* Martin Bormann?"

"It was nobody's idea! The fact is that I have to make a living. I have a wife and small children to support and I survive with the little money these women give me."

The agent continued:

"Where were you born, sir?"

"In Bavaria."

"Do you remember your father?"

"I do not like to remember him."

The agent opened a drawer and pulled out a manila folder. He opened it and picked up a fading brown photograph. The agent showed it to him pointing with his finger to the image of a middle-aged man with a thick moustache.

"Was this your father?"

"Yes. That was my father. Where did you get that photograph?"

"Do I have to remind you, sir, that we are not at the *E'Cole de Santé Militaire* of Lyon? Or at suite 68 of the Terminus Hotel. The war is over. We are in Berlin and I ask the questions."

They remained silent for a moment. Then the agent spoke again with a very soft voice:

"Was your father a school teacher?"

"Yes."

"Was he strict?"

"He was a good German."

"Did he have vices? Did he enjoy bringing salted fish to the prostitutes of Bad Godesborg?"

"My father was a perfect gentleman! The father of a *Sicherheitsdienst* officer could not have vices."

"And an officer of the *Sicherheitsdienst,* like you, has the right to shoot prisoners without reason? Please, explain that to me."

"I don't have the right; but I have the obligation if I have the order to do that."

"Oh... I see."

The agent continued:

"I know that your father was a heavy drinker. Did he ever drink until losing his wits or falling unconscious?"

"All Germans have to drink what they have to. No more no less."

The agent made another gesture of surprise. Then he continued:

"Did he punish his pupils harshly when he went drunk to school?"

"Yes."

"How did he do that?"

"He beat them with his belt. If someone did not do the homework, he punished the entire class. He finished drinking his beer and ran towards them as if he was attacking the French trenches of Verdun. He swung his belt to both sides without caring who was hurt. The lashes passed over their heads, hit the desks and struck the walls. He terrified them. They ran screaming with fear calling for their mothers. They wanted to escape; but they could not. They pushed chairs and desks and ended up trapped against the wall. Some wetted their pants."

"How charming, indeed."

"Breathing heavily, he stopped and rested on a chair staring at his students, one by one. Once he recovered, he made signs for them to return to their seats. As soon as they sat down, he stood up and attacked them with his belt again, screaming. *"Ich greife an!"* (I attack!)

"What a fine man. Extraordinary! Was that his teaching technique?"

"Yes."

"I am utterly astonished... I never knew that such a wonderful technique existed. Did you ever see your father cry?"

"Yes; but he cried because of the pain caused by the French."

"Is that why you hated the French so much?"

"Hatred is the virtue of the strongest. You have to hate your enemy with all your might. You have to despise them. You have to stomp on them and smash them and crush their heads as if they were scorpions."

"Are you the strongest?"

"Can't you see?" answered Klaus standing and intoning, with a soft voice, the first line of the *Horst Wessel*.

"*Die Fahne hoch ... die Reihen fest geschlossen...*"

The agent stared at him serenely. Then he said:

"You get carried away very easily, sir... Do you also softly sing that hymn, when you are getting clients for the women of the *Puttkamerstrasse*?"

"No."

"Do you approach your prospective clients humming that song and showing them your Iron Cross?"

"No."

"Such a pity. You could've been more productive. Let's continue. Are you married?"

"Yes."

"What was the name of the lover you had in Lyon?"

Surprised, Klaus kept quiet. Then he said:

"Odette."

"The secretary of Colonel Fritz Harteck?"

"Yes."

The agent searched inside the envelope for more photographs until he found one in which Odette appeared smiling, with her hair in two black buns, a flowery dress with shoulder pads and a simple necklace.

"Is this Odette?"

"Yes."

"Beautiful lady... French..."

The agent coldly looked at Klaus and asked:

"Did she like the *Irish way*?"

"What do you mean?"

"Never mind. It doesn't matter... Now tell me... How was her *aunt Annie*? Hot?"

"I still don't understand."

"Of course, of course... What I want to know, sir, is if Odette was a passionate woman. In other words, did she like giving *fellatio*?"

Klaus raised completely flushed. He tried to strike the agent; but he blocked his punch quickly and said:

"An unnecessary show of emotion, sir. No argument enders here, mind you? It wouldn't be good for you... So, please, sit down."

Klaus calmed down and returned to his seat slowly. The agent continued:

"Where is Odette?"

"I don't know."

"Don't you know? Sir, you killed her in Lyon!"

"I don't know anything about that."

"When you killed her, sir, didn't you know that she was pregnant?"

"No."

"I'll ask you again. In your last day in Lyon, when everybody was burning documents and forcing their way towards the bridges, didn't you know that she was pregnant?"

"No. I didn't know."

The agent showed him another photo where Odette appeared with untidy hair, naked, lying on the bed. Klaus was behind her. The agent asked:

"Who is this lady?"

Klaus flushed again and answered infuriated:

"Who took this photo? Who did this? It had to be Goebbels. Or Martin Bormann. It was Bormann. I knew it. He was jealous of me because I dismantled the French Resistance. Now you are going to show this photo to my wife... *Das ist ja fürchterlich!*" (That is terrible!)

"You have not answered me, sir... Who is the person who appears in this photograph?"

Klaus thought for a moment; then he said:

"Odette, of course..."

"Wasn't she the attractive French woman who danced with you the *Rosamunde* during the parties at the Terminus Hotel?"

"Yes, she was."

"Do you remember that night?"

"Yes. I do."

The interrogator vocalized a melody:

"Rosamunde, schenk' mir dein Herz und sag' ja!
Rosamunde, frag' doch nicht erst die Mama!
Rosamunde, glaub' mir, auch ich bin dir treu..."

"Yes, yes, yes," interrupted Klaus.

"Wasn't she the one who made love to you, in front of your own soldiers, when you were torturing a member of the French Resistance?"

Klaus stared imperturbably at the interrogator.

The agent said, smiling:

"I have no objections in hearing you..."

Both remained silent, looking at each other. The British agent continued:

"Odette was found dead with a shot to the head after you escaped from Lyon."

"........."

"No voice? No sound? Silence sings like music to my ears."

"........."

"Very well, sir, then tell me. Where is the automatic pistol, the Walther P38, which you used to shoot her?"

"........."

"Don't you remember that to eliminate her you used a Walther P38, 9 mm caliber, bluish steel, with a manual lock, black grips and a double action trigger? A Pistolen P38 like the ones all the Nazi officers had."

"I don't know anything about that. I didn't shoot anyone."

"You, like me, are a soldier," continued the British agent. "I also know what a battlefield is. I fought in the Battle of El Alamein. I defeated Rommel and his troops. I saw his soldiers running away from the frontline, completely undressed... Incandescent deserts... Tanks in flames... Boxes full of bullets... Long live the Queen! Short pants... Oh, Lord! I can recall so clearly that what I see in my mind is too hard to bear. They can tell me anything; but no one will convince me that I have not been to the frontline..."

"............"

"And you are trying to prove to me that you don't know what the parts of a Pistolen P38 are?"

The British agent kept silent for a moment. Then he showed another image:

"Who is this?"

"I don't know. I've never seen him."

"This was Max... Jean Moulin... You assassinated him in Lyon."

"I did not assassinate anyone!"

"This photo was taken three days before you arrested him at Dr. Dugoujon's house. He looks very strong with his hat and scarf. Look how happily he smiles. Completely healthy. Untouched."

Klaus observed with disgust.

The agent showed him another photograph.

"This one was taken after you killed him, when he was being transported to Berlin by train. His face was unrecognizable. Don't you remember the whistling of the locomotive, the creaking of its wheels?"

"I didn't kill him."

"Who killed him then? Al Capone? Or Beowulf? What do you say?"

"............"

The agent pulled out the last photograph. Odette and Klaus were naked, sitting on a bed after love making. She was terrified and crying. He had an automatic pistol pressed to her head.

"What can you tell me about this?"

Klaus became angry again.

"This is another photographic trick!"

"Look at it well. Concentrate on this image, sir. Do you remember this Walther P38? Can you see it? The tip of the steel cannon. Here. Can't you see it? The decoking lever, here. The black grippers. Your finger on the trigger. Her forehead, full of sweat. Look at her. Poor little one. She was trembling with fear. She was terrified! And you pulled the trigger at that moment. Do you remember now?"

"I don't remember anything."

"Who fired this Walther P38, then? Theodoric the Great? Or Alberich the dwarf?"

"It went off by itself."

"You didn't fire. It was the gun that went off by itself..."

"Yes, exactly. That is how it was. I didn't kill her."

There was a moment of silence. Then the agent spoke:

"You may remain silent forever, sir. You may deny everything. But I am utterly convinced that you killed her. And this morning you were trying to convince that little school boy that he was about to have the greatest experience of his life with that *Puttkamerstrasse* woman?"

"............"

"You are perfectly abominable, sir. Indeed..."

"............"

"The deed is done. So, could you please, entertain me now with the first strophe of the *Horst Wessel*? Could you sing it for me, please?"

14

STEAMSHIP CORRIENTES

France wished to bring Klaus to justice, for the torture and death of thousands of innocent civilians. No one could conceal his crimes any longer. He had to be extradited from Germany and brought to the courts in Paris. However, the CIC protected him. The Central Intelligence Corps hired him after he submitted a complete report on the arrest of René Hardy. They found him to be a very clever interrogator and a very good informant on Soviet activities in Berlin. His situation became critical when the French Tribunals trialed René Hardy for treason and demanded Klaus's immediate extradition from occupied Germany. However, his superiors were convinced that if they delivered him to France, the entire world would soon know everything about the CIC. They decided to send him to Bolivia, together with his family, to begin a new life.

A CIC agent escorted him from Augsburg to Genoa and left him on the steamship *Corrientes*, bound to Argentina, on a third class trip. Coming aboard by the gangway, carrying his suitcases, Klaus and his family saw the ship's big chimney painted in red and black, and the ox eyes, with thick glass and round copper frames, on the sides of the vessel. The only war trophies he brought with him were his reddish brown M1934 belt with an aluminum buckle, a *Meldekartentasche,* which he used to carry campaign maps and his Iron Cross.

During the trip over the Atlantic, he met other *S.S.* officers who were going to find safety in South America. Also traveling among them was General Hans Herbert Auerbach, who had come with two chests full of tools to perform his magic tricks. They spent all their time in the lounge, drinking beer and reliving their war exploits. As they had done before, when they attended the parties at the Terminus Hotel, they played the piano and sung German songs like *Gute Nacht Mutter, Mutterlied, Auf Fahrt und Walz, Schön ist die Nacht, Dorothee* and *Märchen und Liebe*. It was like in the good old days. Once drunk, the officers did not have any reservations in giving each other the Nazi salute. Klaus would raise his arm, click his heels and exclaim vigorously. *"Heil Hitler!"* The others answered in the same manner.

When they were quite inebriated, Klaus led them to the bridge. As during the times of the Third Reich, he made them march, some of them staggering, raising their glasses of beer, between rolls of ropes and chains, from one handrail to the other. He led them from the stern to the bow, thrilled by patriotism, as when they had marched across the *Lustgarten*, in front of the Berlin Cathedral. The other passengers smiled and watched them with amazement. Klaus made them sing the *Horst Wessel*, very softly at first and then, with all their energy. Moving over the Atlantic Ocean, the steamship *Corrientes* resounded with this song and with their exclamations.

In the middle of the merrymaking, General Auerbach invited them to put twelve handcuffs and shackles on his wrists and ankles, and several heavy chains around his chest. Then he asked them to throw him over the handrails into the sea. Very excitedly, the drunk ex-officers did as he requested.

The General fell into the ocean with a big splash and disappeared. The expectant passengers watched the water, waiting for him to come out. After a couple of minutes, the ex-officers began to worry and became very serious. After five minutes, Klaus felt very uncomfortable and prepared himself to jump into the sea. However, at that moment, General Auerbach appeared behind them, soaking wet, with his white hair dripping, holding his heavy chains, handcuffs and shackles. Lifting one arm, he screamed, still gasping for air. *"Heil Hitler!"* The officers turned around and seeing that he was alive and well, shouted with joy. They embraced him and carried him around. Then they went back to the lounge looking for more beer and continued the celebration with their favorite songs.

The captain of the *Corrientes*, with a binocular in his hands, did not do anything. Simply looked at his assistants and said: "The Germans are happy today. Leave them alone. Don't bother them."

15

IVAN GONZALEZ

After several months of a violent campaign during the Spanish Civil War, still stunned by the intensity of the pro-Franco's artillery, Ivan González returned, on a short vacation, to his native town of Orihuela. Although with a serious, distrustful and vigilant face, he wanted to swim in the calm waters of the Segura River, dry off in the sun and see the curved trunks and the wide leaves of the distant palms. He missed the rugged hills that surround the ruins of the Orihuela Castle Wall, where during his childhood, sweating and full of happiness, with the bustle and clamor of the other *yuntero* kids, he had played Moors and Christians, fencing with swords made of dry sticks, giving free rein to his imagination, thinking at moments that he was the brave Cid Campeador and the others, his hostile enemies, the Moors. Ivan remembered that during his violent participation in the battlefield, he constantly missed the old Casino Español, on Calderon de la Barca Street, where he had once heard to Miguel Hernández, with his unshaved face and his hoarse voice, reciting one of his best poems.

When he was getting close to town, with the sunset already falling upon him, he spotted the quiet river and the shrubs reflecting on its surface. He vividly reminisced that afternoon when he had gone fishing with his friend Ramon Sijé. He recalled the style of their hair combed backwards, the clothes they used during that day and his neighbors' voices who, between laughter and exclamations, threw their lines into the water. But, what he recollected very vividly was the image of his mother, with her abundant black hair and her serious eyes. He remembered her cutting the brown pig ears and the reddish bacon with its white fat, which she was going to use to prepare an *arròs amb fesols i naps* the day he departed to the battlefield. At that moment his throat tightened and he thought he was going to sob, but he controlled himself.

Ivan arrived to Orihuela dressed with a brown republican uniform, which had small interlaced leather buttons, a woolen beret on his head and a folded blanket across his chest. He wore riding breeches and black boots covered in mud. His *morral* was full of bullets. He carried his Lee-Einfeld rifle on his shoulder and had two hand grenades pinned to his belt. His face was unshaven and dusty. He was delighted to hear the goats bleating, and the red hens scurrying from side to side.

When he saw Jacinto's cabin, he advanced with long steps, grasping his rifle with an unpleasant abhorrence he had never felt before. At that moment, he did not have any interest in Garcia Lorca's poetry or in how Vicente Aleixandre had written his *Song to a Dead Girl*. Instead, he felt that anger and hatred flooded his mind, as when he had fought hand-to-hand with the Nationalists. The sun was almost completely sunken on the red gray horizon.

At that instant he thought he had seen General Francisco Franco followed by three of his soldiers, advancing and hiding behind Jacinto's cabin. "How could it be General Franco?," he asked himself. "Here?" However, it was Franco. Ivan saw him very clearly, with a brown standard military service cap on his head and a black revolver in his hand. Although it was getting darker Ivan recognized the General's small and robust body, his belt across his chest and his clean uniform. He observed his black mustache and his serene face, full of peace, giving orders with short movements of his hand holding the gun. Ivan's eyes became turbid with hatred. He cocked his rifle, ready to open fire.

When he came close to the cabin he kicked the door and opened it violently. He stepped back and called in a loud and angry voice:

"Jacinto!"

Strengthening his black boots on the mud, he accommodated the rifle butt on his shoulder and called again.

As he had done during an assault on a pro-Franco position at the Sanctuary of the *Virgen de la Cabeza* in Andujar, he aimed fixedly towards the door watching through the sight, ready to pull the trigger.

Wiping his hands with a white cloth Jacinto emerged and despite the increasing darkness he recognized Ivan. He was astonished to see him with a gun aimed at him and immediately he understood what was going to happen. Nevertheless, he regained his composure and putting his hands on his hips, slowly walked in front of Ivan as when one walks before an angry bull and asked:

"What's the matter, Ivan?"

"Kneel down, Jacinto!"

Jacinto felt that his throat had suddenly dried and that the hair of his neck was standing. He took two steps backwards and tried to dissuade him.

"Take that rifle away from me, Ivan. I am innocent."

"Kneel down, Jacinto!," Ivan said looking fixedly at his face with the Lee-Enfield rifle. Jacinto felt that his hands had become cold and clammy. Nevertheless, he tried to discourage him.

"Don't be silly, Ivan. God is seeing us from above. Never kill anyone in the presence of the Lord."

"On your knees!"

"Wait, Ivan, wait! Don't you believe in God? What did the priests teach you when you were *un chavalillo*?"

"You should know that I do not believe in God or in any of your lies. I am a republican!"

With a trembling voice, Jacinto replied:

"Don't be a heretic, Ivan! How can you talk like that?"

"Do you also believe that God was looking at you when you reported my mother to the *Guardia Civil*?"

The eyes of Jacinto filled with panic. Stammering he said:

"Hey, wait! It was not my fault. They executed your mother because she was a republican, like you. I did not expose her! They knew where she was. They came and shot her, bang!"

"I come from hell, Jacinto. If I did not see the devil, it was because he became scared with the noise of the machine guns and the whistling of the bullets and hid behind the debris and the bombarded buildings. I come from the ruins of the Bank of Spain. I left the battle of Teruel, fighting hand-to-hand. Now, you want me to believe that you are innocent? Long live the Republic! Long live freedom! Run Jacinto!"

"What did you say?"

"I told you to run. Escape! Run in zigzag. *Que m'entens?*"

"Why do I have to run? I was not the one, Ivan. Are you crazy?"

"*Som-hi!* Run!"

"Why? I didn't do anything."

"Don't ask me why, idiot. Just run!"

"Where?"

"Wherever you want, *botabancals*. Now!," exclaimed Ivan very furious, almost with desperation. "Run, imbecile! Escape!"

Finally, Jacinto seemed to understand and a sign of hope appeared in his eyes. He turned around and ran. He ran at full speed, zigzagging by the side of his house. For a moment he stumbled; but he kept dashing from side to side.

It was dark already when a powerful shot resounded in the valley, but Jacinto continued moving. Another explosion followed and the body of Jacinto staggered

94

and soon it fell forward. Ivan cautiously approached the fallen one. He touched his throat to verify that the man was without life.

Staring at all directions, he observed in the distance the dark silhouettes of the palms and the hills of the *Oriolana* Mountains. He turned around and walked away with long strides, with the rifle in his hands; but suddenly he remembered the crime committed against his mother and his detestation intensified. He stomped over the wet soil with his black boot and sobbed for a second. But he refrained himself and watching at the place where his adversary had fallen, he experienced again an uncontrollable repugnance. Making a gesture of contempt, he unhooked a hand grenade from his belt and pulled out the pin with his teeth. He waited for a few seconds and then threw it towards Jacinto. A great yellow reddish explosion illuminated the entire place accompanied by an uproarious sound. Almost reflexively, he bent down, to protect himself from whatever could fall on top of him. But the detonation pushed Ivan into the mud. He rose quickly and wiped his hands on his pants, cleaned his rifle and turned around. He could not see anything in the place his adversary had fallen. With his Lee-Enfield rifle on his shoulder, in complete darkness, listening to the crickets chirp, he walked rapidly towards the outskirts of town, and softly began to sing the *Quinto Regimiento*:

> *Con el quinto, quinto, quinto*
> *Con el quinto regimiento.*
> *Madre, yo me voy p'al frente*
> *Para las líneas de fuego.*
> *Anda jaleo, jaleo*
> *Suena una ametralladora*
> *Y ya empieza el tiroteo*
> *y ya empieza el tiroteo.*

Now, Ivan lives in Quirio, a town located at forty kilometers to the East of the city of Lima, near the house of Manuelita Sanchez and her father. Following the advice of the secretary general of his political party to protect the Spanish republicans who had come to take refuge in Peru, Anselmo Sanchez accepted to see after the expatriate as if he were a relative. Now Ivan spends his time playing with the tin toys that belonged to Manuelita's brother before he died during his childhood. There are also tanks, jeeps and airplanes. Sometimes, leaning on the floor, submerged in deep thoughts, illuminated by the intense sun light that enters through the door and showing a great excitement in his eyes, Ivan displays the numerous tin soldiers, as Republicans and Nationalists and moves them recreating all the actions of the battles in which he participated.

In Lima, he has found another kind of poetry. Verses of *Trilce* and *España, Aparta de Mi Este cáliz* by Cesar Vallejo. He has read them, reliving all what happened in the battlefield. He has also reviewed *La Casa de Cartón* by Martín Adán, *Tradiciones* by Ricardo Palma, *Blanca Sol* by Mercedes Cabello de Carbonera and *Birds Without a Nest* by Clorinda Matto de Turner. Recently he has finished *Los Ríos Profundos* by José María Arguedas.

16

IN THE NEW CONTINENT

The steamship *Corrientes* arrived in Buenos Aires on April, 1951. The smell of the *asados, chorizos* and *longanizas* as well as the melody of the tangos and milongas enchanted Klaus and his family. Especially the sharp and potent sound of the *bandoneones* and the violins. After discovering the sincerity and the nobility of the Argentinians, he wished he would have been exiled to *Rio de la Plata*; but the CIC orders had to be followed and the trip continued.

General Hans Auerbach promptly found a job in a traveling German circus. Frequently at night he worked with his shiny golden clothes, swallowing sabers and removing shackles and bracelets from his hands and feet. Smiling, with his long white hair, he used to saw a coffin in half without harming the beautiful young woman enclosed in it. He also worked as a lion tamer, cracking his whip and making the felines jump through three big rings of fire under the dramatic accompaniment of the band's music. He was one of the first magicians, who made the act of making a ferocious lion disappear from one cage to reappear yawning in a distant cage.

Six days later, Klaus and his family went to the railroad station and bought tickets for a trip to Bolivia. In a train pulled by a locomotive with a bright copper *cowcatcher*, they continued their journey to La Paz. In this city, they stayed at the Italy Hotel. Its interior, for some reason, was reminiscent of the Terminus Hotel in Lyon. But it was very close to restaurants and coffee shops, from where they could admire the Illimani, covered by snow. Not accustomed to the altitude, the mountain sickness affected them. He felt weary and had constant headaches which he cured attaching wet coca leaves to his forehead as a native had advised him. His wife noticed palpitations whenever she climbed stairs or when she moved too fast. She became frantic because she thought she had acquired a heart malady. During a social gathering organized by the Club La Paz, he realized that he could not dance with the same energy as when he had jitterbugged with Odette in the Hotel Royal, whistling and clapping under the tune of a Lyonnais band. Despite these initial difficulties, he went out looking for employment; but he did not find any. He survived with the money borrowed from his new German friends.

For a moment, Klaus contemplated the possibility of mugging defenseless Bolivians, as he had done when he arrested innocent civilians in Amsterdam, to steal their wrist watches and sell them in the black market. He also thought of finding clients for the local prostitutes as he had done in the Alexanderplatz area when the British Intelligence Service was very interested in finding him. However he promptly understood that the Bolivian reality was a different one and he had to do things in a new way.

He kept looking for employment. One of those days when he was strolling through the streets of La Paz, he saw a parade organized by the Socialist Bolivian Phalanx. He felt elated when he discovered that the Falangists were *Paceño* Indians dressed in Nazi uniforms, holding vermilion banners with silver swastikas surrounded by golden crowns. He heard familiar hymns and for a moment he thought he was parading at the *Luitpoldhain* of Nuremberg. He almost broke into tears and applauded with immense enthusiasm following the marching Falangists until the parade ended. Then everybody dispersed and he was left alone on the street again with his palms still clasped together, but without anyone to clap for.

Fortunately for him, Hans Ertl, a German photographer and filmmaker, who had worked as a journalist in North Africa, covering the campaign of Marshal Erwin Rommel, found a job for him. It was a position as a sawmill administrator, in Caranavi, Bolivia's forest paradise. Although he did not know anything about cutting trees, he accepted the post and with his family moved there. Since he did not know how to speak the Spanish language, during his first labor day, he made the workers, carrying their tools, stand in line in a military position as if they were an *Einsatzcommando*. He spoke to them in German, like a Nazi officer addressing his soldiers before going into battle. He explained the goals of the National Socialism and the Führer's plans to conquer the world.

"Heute werden... wir eine... Seite der Geschichte schreiben...," he said.

Then, slapping a mosquito off his face, he sang a Nazi hymn. His workers did not understand anything. Astonished, they thought that their new foreman was insane and decided to remain silent and let the time pass.

Realizing that the laborers did not comprehend him, Klaus decided to change his tactics. He spoke with great fondness with the few words in Spanish he knew. By signs, he indicated that it was time to cut the trees. Then the men raised the saws and the axes and walked towards the nearby forest.

During those days, they informed him that a military court in Lyon had sentenced him to death for the murders and massacres he had committed against innocent civilians in the Montluc prison and the Bron airport. When he learned that the French Army had hung him, *in absence,* a chill ran from his nape down to his tailbone. Thinking about how he would look inside a coffin after being dead for a month, he became horrified and felt like passing out. He tried to gather courage and exclaimed. *"Heil Hitler!"* However, his clamor sounded like the trembling scream of a newborn.

Soon he bought his own sawmill. He left the business in charge of an associate and traveled to La Paz in search for clients, but he found none. At that time, no one was interested in buying wood and his trees begun to pile up around his office in Caranavi. Fortunately for him, Friederich Schwend, another Nazi exiled in Peru, invited him to come to Lima to work for the military government. The Peruvian regime needed an experienced Gestapo interrogator who could extract information from communist insurgents. His assignment consisted of questioning political prisoners, especially leftist guerrillas incarcerated in the Fronton Island. He would use the same skills he had used in Lyon, and would conduct his interrogations in the same manner he had done at the Terminus Hotel and the Montluc prison.

During those days in La Paz, Klaus learned that agents of the *Mossad* had kidnapped Adolf Eichmann in Buenos Aires. It happened while Klaus was eating the delicious meat of a *salteña* with black olives, fragments of hard boiled eggs and several lemon drops, in a fashionable restaurant, at eleven o'clock in the morning. His bodyguard showed him the front page of a newspaper where Eichmann, with a bright monocle in one eye, appeared smiling.

Adolf Eichmann had begun his career as an officer of the *Schutzstaffel* at the concentration camp of Dachau. However, soon he found this employment monotonous and requested his transfer to the *Sicherheitsdienst*. There he worked gathering information about prominent Jews. Meticulously he learned all the aspects of the Hebrew culture, attended Jewish celebrations and sang with them with a *yarmulke* on his head. He took notes and made sketches while visiting synagogues. He became fluent in the Yiddish language and turned into a specialist on Judaic matters. In Austria, he established the *Zentralstelle fuer juedische Auswanderung* that made possible for Jewish families to escape from Germany after forfeiting all their properties to the Third Reich.

The always clean and neat *Obersturmbanführer* Adolf Eichmann accepted the responsibility of sending all the Jewish population of Europe to the concentration camps of Treblinka and Auschwitz-Birkenau. In the last one, with his seraphic and spiritual face, he chose the place for the gas chambers. After examining dozens of bottles with different poisons, he authorized the use of Zyklon-B, while saying in low voice: *"Wunderbare...,"* as the best lethal agent to carry out the operation with efficiency and swiftness.

During an Autumn evening, Eichmann observed in person, with his aquiline nose and his eyes full of tenderness and kindness, holding a monocle in one eye, the quick *gasification* of two hundred victims. Once the process had concluded, always in good mood, Eichmann went to the kitchen, to enjoy the delightful *Hasenpfeffer* prepared for dinner. Dr. Josef Mengele, joined him, laughing and constantly quoting Nazi slogans. He commented on the medical experiments he had carried away lately with a few joyous twins and a few boisterous dwarfs who had arrived at the camp two days earlier.

After the collapse of the Third Reich, Eichmann escaped from Berlin and lived underground for several months. With the help of a secret organization, he moved to Argentina. There he lived undisturbed for ten years, cleaning the floor of a factory with a mop and a bucket of water, under the false name of Ricardo Klement. Other times he labored as a water engineer during the day and as a very diligent rat catcher during the night. Very often, the *Obersturmbanführer* could be seen in the basement, lifting a mouse by the tail, illuminating it with his flashlight and staring very surprised at it with a monocle in one eye. Everything went well for him until a Mossad commando identified him and captured him near his house on Garibaldi Street.

Although he offered a fierce resistance at the beginning, throwing jabs, uppercuts and overhands, changing steps and moving his head, as if he were a fighter shadow boxing in a ring, while shouting threatening Nazi insults, the strongest of the Israeli agents grabbed him from the ankles and lifted him up, saying: "*Krystalnicht* is over!" Hanging upside down like a timid rabbit, Eichmann, one of the last specimens of the *superior race*, lost all hopes of living in freedom and flexed his arms and hands. He surrendered without further resistance. After his arrest, they transported him out of Buenos Aires in an Israeli airplane. Upon his arrival to Jerusalem, David Ben Gurion announced the news to the Knesset and to the world.

Upon seeing the newspaper, Klaus almost choked on his *salteña* and coughed. He dropped over the plate the newspaper with the photo of Eichmann in Nazi uniform. His bodyguard approached him, and gave him a few thumps on the back and supported his forehead.

"Klaus! Klaus! What happened? Speak to me! Are you all right?"

Klaus continued coughing, very flushed, with bulging eyes, inhaling air with difficulty, but he coughed for the last time and calmed down. He thought that if the Mossad was going to kidnap him in La Paz or in Lima he had to wear anklets with iron spikes, so it will be more difficult for his captors to catch him.

17

SPANISH REPUBLICANS IN LIMA

When the Spanish Republicans arrived to the town of Quirio, near Lima, Manuelita Sánchez and her father helped them find a place to live. They accommodated Ivan González in a house damaged by an earthquake. He arrived wearing the same uniform he had used during the Spanish Civil War and felt very comfortable walking around with his woolen cap and his brown jacket with leather buttons. He enjoyed wearing his riding pants, his black boots and his dagger in its scabbard. Several years earlier the earthquake had destroyed the house assigned to him. It had lost the top half. For this reason, it reminded Ivan of the bombarded buildings where he had been during the battle of Teruel. However, the place was still in livable conditions.

He stayed there with his wife, a good-looking and always smiling *ilicitana,* who liked to cook *Tortillas a la Española*. She also enjoyed simmering *altaballacos, gachasmigas* and *guisados de albondigas*. For the Advent season she fried *paparajotes* in a pan full of cotton oil and for Christmas, she baked *toñas*. Every Sunday, the aroma of rice with saffron, garlic, shrimp, mussels, sausage and pork of the *Paella a la Valenciana*, dispersed all over Quirio.

With the passage of time, Ivan developed a great friendship with Anselmo Sánchez and became like a second father to Manuelita. He amused her by describing his life during the war. In that way, Manuelita learned that Ivan had met the poet Miguel Hernández when he came to Orihuela, to marry Josefina Manresa. The renowned bard also attended the intellectual gatherings held in the Casino Español, located on Calderon de la Barca Street. There, dressed in his military uniform, Hernández read one of his most delightful works. He arrived as a Culture Delegate of *El Campesino* Battalion. From that time, they corresponded from Orihuela to the front and exchanged verses. Ivan was so impressed with Hernández that he decided to also be a soldier-poet and enrolled in the Fifth Regiment.

The Republican also narrated some joyous situations that occurred during the war. He remembered the occasion when they went over the Nationalist frontline to capture one of Franco's soldiers and bring him in for interrogation. They crossed the river and captured a *franquista* who was absentmindedly relieving himself in the water. Despite the intense shooting, they returned without incidents.

Soon they realized that they had brought a soldier who was a good-natured man, who smiled even when his life was in danger. The prisoner also knew the lieutenant who was going to do the interrogation. "Cousin!" exclaimed the *franquista* as soon as the republican entered the room, lit up only by a small lamp. "Santiago!" answered the other. "Where have you been, *coño*? I haven't seen you for such a long time."

There was no cross-interrogation. Instead, they drank wine and talked about their lives. Despite the terrifying noise and the trembling due to the nearby bombardment, the *Nationalist* said that he was a *rejoneador* and that he was always in bad mood because he had married a beautiful woman who looked like Ava Gardner, the movie star. For that reason, all their neighbors wooed her, on Sundays, when he was working at the bullring. If he brought her to the *coso*, those who importuned her were the spectators sitting next to her. All the *matadors* dedicated their *faenas* to her. It was so uncomfortable for him to see, from his horse, that all male eyes were on his wife, and not on the bullfighting, unless the bull was hurting someone.

As for Ivan, sometimes he had the frightening sensation that he had seen General Franco and three of his soldiers in Quirio, walking by the neighboring houses. He saw them staring at him with angry eyes, uttering filthy words in Spanish and making insulting gestures with their hands. "Son of a bitch! You will see when I catch you. *Te cortaré los cojones!*" (I will cut off your balls!) One of them, the lieutenant with the *requetés andaluz*, passed his hand across his throat very slowly, indicating that Ivan was already dead. Those were very intimidating moments. When that happened, Ivan felt dominated by fear. Cold sweat covered his forehead. Quickly, he hid wherever he could with his hands clutching an imaginary rifle and thinking on how he could defend himself. When he was about to scream, his fear evanesced gradually and he became serene and composed. Then he understood that everything had been the work of his mind.

Other times, while having lunch with Mercedes, Iván had the feeling that people were singing on the street an old Franquist song he had heard during the war:

"Facing the sun, with the shirt that you embroidered yesterday…"

He became alarmed, pushed his plate aside and leaned backwards on his chair trying to listen with more attention:

"… Death will find me and I will not see you again…"

He rose with much alarm and walked briskly towards the window. But the street was empty and quiet. Nevertheless the song continued in his mind.

At that instant, he realized that the singers were going away slowly until he did not hear them anymore. On other occasions he dreamt that several legionaries, with their green caps and baggy trousers, and their leather leggings, jumped through the window, entered the room where he was sleeping and shot him at point-blank with their Mausers, in the middle of a dense cloud of gun powder-smelling smoke. The firing was so nerve-racking that he woke up screaming with panic and aroused his wife. After sweating profusely and breathing anxiously he calmed down gradually. Then he said to her:

"Mercedes! I didn't have more bullets…"

Anselmo Sánchez molded Manuelita's political vocation at an early age. He was a construction worker and a proud militant since the year of the insurrection in the city of Trujillo. He always remembered that Colonel Sánchez Cerro, a great admirer of Hitler, had ordered the execution of one thousand striking workers from the Cartavio and Laredo *haciendas*. He had done this as a retaliation for rebelling against the government and for assassinating fifty Army officers. There were no summary trials. The firing squads executed them with old machine guns, which the Iglesias Division had used in the defense of the Morro Solar during the Pacific War.

Since an early age, Manuelita accompanied her father in marches and rallies, through the streets and plazas of Lima, holding banners and chanting slogans. On several occasions, she had witnessed clashes between the strikebreaking police and the workers. She recalled the day when the cavalrymen attacked the unarmed demonstrators, slashing them with their swords. She saw them, with fierce gestures, galloping towards them at full speed. The protesters dropped their banners and ran searching for a refuge. At that moment the horses slipped over the wet streetcar rails and glided over the asphalt, neighing with their empty saddles and their raised heads. She remembered hearing the metallic sound of the savers sliding over the wet ground. Some laborers remained lying down, dead or wounded; others screamed and asked for mercy. A journalist, in order to demonstrate the brutality of the repressive forces, published in his newspaper a photograph of Manuelita, in which she appeared as a sad and innocent-looking girl, with a large bandage around her head and blood covering her face.

18

KLAUS IN LIMA

What Klaus liked most about Lima was the Portal of Plaza San Martin. There he enjoyed reading the newspaper while drinking a cup of delicious Chanchamayo coffee. At the same time, the bootblacks with their brushes, pomades and rags did their best to make his shoes shine. He also liked *Campo de Marte*, an extensive and open area. It seemed ideal to him for a military parade with tanks, cavalry and roaring biplanes passing over the watching crowds. Like the one in which he and the *Sturm Abteilung* participated, lifting their boots the highest they could, singing the *Horzt Wessel*, in front of the *Neue Wache* building of Berlin, on March of 1938.

Klaus enjoyed going to the Crillón Restaurant with his German friends to drink *pisco sour*, with its layer of cinnamon on top and the lemon slice hanging from the edge of the glass. Smiling all the time, he was the prototypical successful businessman. *Ceviche* with *choclos* and sweet potatoes became his favorite dish. The pungency of the *ceviche* juice reminded him of the *Saumon Aigrelette* that Odette liked so much, when they went out to dine at the restaurants and night clubs of Lyon, after torturing the members of the French Resistance. The hot peppers, to which he had become accustomed in Bolivia, became his delight. He chewed their seeds and swallowed them with a gulp of beer. He also enjoyed the flavor of the cilantro in the *arroz con pato*, the exquisite flavor of the pork and dry potatoes of the *carapulcra* and the savory *olluquito con charqui*.

His wife was never present. Instead, he was fond of bringing Kassandra, his lover. She was a spectacular Cuban female, tall and slender, extremely beautiful and a champion of the mambo dance. She particularly liked to step, making her shoulders and her magnificent buttocks shudder and tremble, under the saxophone rhythm of the orchestra and the blowing of the trumpets. *"Maaambó! Que rico el mambo! Eh, eh, eh!"* She was the kind of woman who enjoyed drinking rum with Coca-Cola while listening to old and melancholic songs by Leo Marini. Songs like *Maringá, Cobardía* and *Caribe Soy*. Her appearance and her seducing way of walking frequently attracted all the male eyes in Lima's nightclubs. Sometimes, to the annoyance of Klaus, she had to hear a long, unexpected and passionate whistling. She was very religious, a devotee of the *Virgen del Cobre* and a prayer of rosaries on Fridays. There was also the insisting rumor that she liked to dance mambo, completely undressed, except for her high heel shoes, in front of Klaus, when they were in private in his Miraflores bungalow.

During those days Frederika, the perfect example of the Teutonic beauty, with her long blond hair and her attractive body, appeared in Lima. She had survived the War and came to Lima with her Kindergarten child. For a while, she worked as a secretary in the German Chamber of Commerce, raising the passion and the expectations of the men who worked there. Later on, after a long and difficult courtship, she married Eugenio Benigno de la Cámara y Fuentesclaras. He was the lucky son of a *miraflorino* tycoon who had made his fortune, selling hair tonics to the bald people of Lima. In the years to come, Frederika's daughter, Hildegard, would make the newspapers highlights. That happened when one of her jealous fiancées shot and killed a Chilean diplomat who obsessively stalked her and wooed her.

By then, General Hans Herbert Auerbach, with his silvery long hair, also appeared in Lima working for a German Circus, during the week of the Independence celebrations. The remainder of the year, with the clowns, the magicians of black tall hats and the trapeze flyers, he traveled on tour, throughout the provinces of the country. While in Lima, the General opened a chicken farm in Vitarte, following the advice of retired Colonel Frederich Schwend. He intended to raise chickens and sell eggs to the local population, after consulting with his daily horoscope. For the management of the new business he hired a one-man-orchestra administrator. He would be in charge of cleaning the farm, conducting the accounting, distributing the goods among the locals, vaccinating the chickens and doing a marketing campaign as effective as a Holland *Blietzkrieg*. He would also be in charge of cleaning and keeping in good shape all his shackles, handcuffs and swords. The selected one was Takeo Ishikawa, a young Japanese immigrant. He was a quiet, very polite and bright young man who immediately accepted his assignments with patience and eagerness. The first thing he did was to clean and grease the shackles and polish the General's swords as if they belonged to an Emperor.

The business of the chicken farm did not prosper as expected because it started on a bad day, according to the Zodiac reading. Actually, the local population grew their own chickens and produced their own eggs. Therefore, when General Auerbach, with his bronzed face and his green eyes, learned that Takeo Ishikawa had been a top *chef* at a luxury hotel in Osaka and knew all about the Japanese cuisine, he decided to open a restaurant. The name would be the Tokyo Delight and it would be located in the high-class areas of Miraflores and San Isidro. Takeo would be in charge of preparing the chicken teriyaki and sushi, Samurai Style. General Auerbach would entertain his customers by cutting two watermelons, with swift strokes, to the right and to the left, with a *Katana*, an ancient Japanese sword. Then, he would swallow the blade without hurting himself. After that, licking the sweet taste on his lips, he would bow and greet his clients.

By that time, the General received a letter from Munich, written by Colonel Fritz Harteck. He mentioned that he was working as a common laborer, with his shoeless feet, cleaning the sewage system of that city. He complained that he still had horrible nightmares in which the French Resistance fighters would appear killing his soldiers by the side of a train bound to Auschwitz. He also had bad dreams in which the Roman emperors would emerge, frightening him out of his wits, walking with lions in front of the statue of Louis XIV, calling him: *"Suevi! Teutoni!"* and demanding an answer for the disappearance of thirty Italian workers, who during the Third Reich, had been sent to an uranium mine to work as war slaves, but had never returned.

Controlling his irascibility, the General advised Colonel Harteck to stop wasting his time with dreams in which the maquis with their machine guns would turn his soldiers into ground beef and in which the lions would bite him and swallow him raw, chewing and licking his bones until nothing was left to see. He also advised him to stop cleaning the sewage of that city. Instead, he urged him to leave Munich at once and come to work at the Tokyo Delight, which was about to open. Colonel Fritz Harteck, the Conqueror of Ain, dressed in military uniform, with his bright medals on his chest and a monocle in one eye, could appear holding his swords, with a long and black cigarette-holder in his lips, while the General would swiftly swallow them one by one in front of the clientele. He could also be of great help in the kitchen, cleaning and gutting the fish for the sushi, Samurai style, steaming rice in the Japanese fashion and preparing *Sake* cups for those inclined to the pleasures of the Far Orient. Besides, the Colonel, who had ordered to hang black signboards with white skulls on the trees of the Ain forest, forbidding the practice of witchcraft and black magic, could help in the kitchen removing, with his dagger adorned with a swastika on the handle, the tails of the shrimps before shaking the prawn tempura in a wooden bucket full of flour. He would also learn to cook flavorful *miso* soups adding the necessary amount of *wakame* seaweed.

Colonel Harteck was the perfect example of the Aryan race, with blond hair and blue eyes. Therefore, unfit to work directly with the local clientele. Nevertheless, his great experience as a commander officer of the *S.D.* forces during the elimination of the French Resistance from Oyonnax would be of great value. Also, as a decorated hero of the Belgium Campaign, he could use his Teutonic efficiency to sweep the floors, clean the tables after the Restaurant had closed, throw away the garbage and prepare everything for the next business day. Despair should not be a reason for a *Sicherheitsdienst* officer to procrastinate. The General strongly suggested his immediate transportation to the city of Lima.

19

THE SEARCH FOR ANSELMO SANCHEZ

When Anselmo failed to come home one night, Manuelita had the frightening suspicion that the German agent, working for the Peruvian Army, had captured him at the *Parque Universitario*, where he used to take the bus every night. The construction worker himself had warned her about this possibility, a few days before, when several of his closest comrades had disappeared without leaving a trace. The next morning, Manuelita went out looking for her father. She asked the *chicharron* seller who did her business one block away from the School of *Bellas Artes*. She inquired in the *chinganas* of Surquillo, the churches of Barrios Altos and the liquor stores in the center of Lima, including the *Panaderia La Virreyna*. She visited old relatives and acquaintances in Barranco and *Abajo el Puente*, but obtained no positive replies. She dropped by *Siete Jeringas* Street, where her godmother lived and went to the Party's central office; but she did not have any answer. No one had seen him or heard from him for several days. Anselmo had simply vanished. Sobbing, she told Ivan about his disappearance. When she finished, the Republican said:

"Manuelita, when someone disappears like this, there are only three possibilities: The hospital, the jail or the cemetery."

They went out immediately in search of Anselmo. Traveling in clunky streetcars and walking through long streets and avenues, among fruit sellers and shoe peddlers, they arrived to a bustling infirmary. There they asked the medical staff and the rude employees for her father, but no one, after looking briskly in their Book of Admissions, gave any satisfactory response. It seemed that everyone was in a hurry and nobody was willing to talk more than was needed.

They left the hospital and decided to visit El Sexto Prison. The attention of the workers there, was even worse. Manuelita and Ivan had to wait in long lines, among noisy relatives, soliciting prostitutes and watchful thieves. They endured the rudeness of the clerks, who refused to give any information. The entire prison seemed to be submerged in an absolute chaos. Unexpectedly, after a worker told them that they had been in the wrong line, a pitiless and brutal guard, with an assault rifle in his hands, ordered them to leave the premises.

It was near the end of the day, when they went to the old *Presbítero Maestro* Cemetery. There, after speaking, in a quiet office, with the representative of the *Public Charity* and the uncouth and defiant gravediggers, no one could give a sound answer. They were all evasive. At the end, to make things worse, one of them suggested that perhaps the administration had sold the still fresh body to the Medical School, so the students could practice during their classes of Human Anatomy. This revelation caused Manuelita severe distress, and she bitterly sobbed in front of everybody. Seeing this, Ivan lost his self-control and scolded the clerk:

"Hey! Shut up! Why do you talk about things that you don't know, eh?"

They left the cemetery with great indignation.

The following day, in a last effort, they went to the Central Morgue of Lima. Fortunately, this time, the detective on duty was kinder. He searched in his files and found news about Anselmo. They had finished his autopsy the day before. The Pathologist's report indicated that the deceased had been ferociously beaten and tortured before dying. The diagnosis was: "Homicide by gunshot wound to the head."

At that moment, Manuelita confirmed what she had suspected for several days and knew immediately who the author of the horrendous crime was. She felt an intense hatred and realized that she had never experienced a similar detestation against anyone else before. She never knew that hatred and anger could reach such a revolting level.

20

ANSELMO'S FUNERAL

Anselmo's funeral was held at his own home in Quirio. Several years earlier, the wake of Manuelita's mother had also taken place in the same room. She recalled the moment when a group of friends were carrying her mother's remains to the cemetery. Anselmo, younger at the time, crying with a white handkerchief to his nose and placing a hand over the black and shiny coffin, asked her beloved to forgive him for being a bad husband. He wanted his wife to pardon him for his philandering and for having so many affairs during their marriage.

The renown striker, the one who disputed the labor contracts, deplored having other women on his own street and twenty-two other sweethearts through out the city. He promised, in loud voice and in front of the pallbearers and the observing crowd, that if his consort could come back to life he would never look at another woman. "My love, forgive me also for being such a jealous husband," he said. He had, frequently and deliriously, displayed violent scenes of jealousy, in front of their neighbors. Completely out of his wits, he accused her of having an affair with the knife-sharpener, who came to the neighborhood to do his business dressed in rags. He also, insanely, accused his wife of flirting with a drunken bottle-buyer, who sometimes fell asleep on top of his own merchandise. Love is as inebriating as jealousy is maddening, he had said once, and both go hand in hand.

Manuelita remembered that after her mother's funeral, Anselmo stayed in the cemetery for two days and two nights, drinking and sobbing, in front of her niche, with a bottle of *pisco* in his hand and a pack of *El Inca* cigarettes, in his pocket. After midnight, terrified with the idea that his wife was too cold and lonely inside her vault, the proud militant had the desire to break its concrete door and remove her from there. He wanted to hug her, hum the songs she liked and tell her how much he loved her. He promised never to accuse her of infidelities again although his jealousy would be chewing and licking his brain. He banged the cemented door of the niche with his two fists, repeatedly, asking her to come out. "Please, don't leave me alone in this world. Without you, I am worthless!" Unable to satisfy his wish, Anselmo, drooling and crying, closed his eyes and sang *The Plebeian*. When he finished the famous song, he stared the golden label of the bottle of *pisco* then drank from its beak without pausing, producing bubbles within the liquor. Breathing heavily, he gulped and gulped until the bottle was empty. He wanted to sing again: *"I'm the Plebeian, the son of the people... the man who knew how to love."* But he couldn't. The bottle fell from his hand and he fainted, falling to the floor and hurting his head.

The following morning, the cemetery guards found him on the ground, as pale as a corpse, shallowly breathing and unconscious. An ambulance took him to the hospital where he remained unresponsive for three days. The moment he opened his eyes and recognized where he was and who he was, he screamed and wailed like a tormented beast.

Now, in his own casket, after an ex-officer of the *Sicherheitzdienzt* tortured and killed him, Anselmo was resting motionless, unable of being a womanizer or a jealous consort. His relatives placed his coffin over a long table covered by a black cloth. There were numerous glowing lamps with foggy crystals. Some of them had the shape of an ardent flame, with its tips upwards; others had the form of a perfect sphere. The light illuminated Anselmo's face and made it shine. His prominent forehead and his aquiline nose seemed paler than usual. With his thin lips and his well trimmed black mustache, he bore a close resemblance to Inca Garcilazo de la Vega.

Behind the glass window of the varnished pine box, everyone could see his serene expression. A burst wound on his cheek revealed the violence used during the interrogation. Undoubtedly, he had lived through an extremely painful experience. His relatives had dressed him with the same white shirt and red tie with green stripes, which he had worn during his stay in the cemetery when he refused to abandon his wife. Abundant white satin adorned the interior giving the impression of being a very comfortable place. A shiny bronze pew was set at its foot for those who wished to pray, but nobody used it. Numerous wreaths made of fragrant red roses, white carnations, yellow gladioli and palm leaves, with condolences cards, were very nearly placed.

After seeing Anselmo, some of the visitors, with a mixture of sadness and fear, wept uncontrollably. "He was tortured," they said. Others mumbled kind words with a concerned face and passed directly to the back room, where there was coffee and crackers with *ancashina* butter and delicious *queso mantecoso*. The guests participated in the conversation of the mourners. Old ghost stories and dirty jokes were the main stock of the colloquy. The visitors exploded in laughter after listening to the tales.

The women sat in the living room, praying their rosaries with lighted candles in their hands. This contrasted with the noise of the other attendants. While the women were devotedly reciting litanies for the soul of Anselmo Sánchez, the men burst in laughter and exhilaration in the backroom after hearing the dirty jokes and the ghost stories. One of the jokers said that members of the family had to watch the deceased during the entire night. Otherwise, the demons would come, puffing, growling and groaning, take the body out of the catafalque and drag it through the streets until arriving to hell, where they would bury it in one of its deepest crevices. One of the other demons, then, would lie down and accommodate himself inside the coffin, waiting for the relatives to see him. He enjoyed when the family members screamed out of sheer panic, after finding him inside the coffin instead of the deceased one.

Another participant, the one who sold *turrones de doña Pepa* in October, said that in the *Callejón de las Siete Puñaladas*, they found one of his dead neighbors, laid to rest several days before, peacefully eating a *chicharrón with salsa criolla,* at the kitchen table. He was joyfully calling his wife to share it with him. When she, still mourning, came to the table and saw her husband eating, she passed out and plunged to the floor. After seeing his beloved wife losing consciousness, he also dropped over his plate. The relatives carried him to another casket and quickly sealed the door and took him to the old Matías Maestro Cemetery.

Another joker, the one with the multicolored Andean woolen cap with ear covers, told the story of a woman, who lived on *Lechugal Street,* in a house with bronze door knockers and Florentine gardens, and who had died after a long agony. Nevertheless, during her wake, after midnight, she aroused from her death, as if awakening from a dream. She tried to get out of her coffin; but in doing so she tumbled down. After remaining reclined on the floor for a while she stood up slowly. Very weak, dragging one leg, she went to her former bedroom to ask her husband if he still loved her. She needed her spouse to tell her every day that he loved her. Upon entering her chamber, she found her venerated and faithful husband, the owner of two slaughterhouses in the streets of Lima and a water mill in a terrain which later would become known as the Pepinal of Ancieta, in a hot love making scene, desperately and violently striking the buttocks of her most dear niece, a beautiful Andalucian, in her favorite position. "Josefina!" the dead woman said to herself. "How could you?" After thinking for a brief moment, she lifted the white sheet with her cold hands, slowly climbed into the bed and laid behind her husband. She slowly passed her hand over his moving hip until she reached his pubic area. Then quietly and gently she caressed and pulled his hairs. She also pulled Josefina's. When the two lovers realized that there was another person in the bed with them, they stopped their love making and sat up. Frightened they saw the gray hairs and the wrinkled and ashen face of the dead woman, who, moving her dry and stiff lips with difficulty, asked him with an agonizing voice: "Do you still love me, Jose Antonio?" With sudden panic, the naked widower, abandoned the dormitory and ran towards the main door. Tripping at moments, with his soul escaping from his mouth, he ran through the streets shrieking with terror. The horrified niece, unable to do anything else, scurried away, covered her breasts with the sheet and screamed full of panic, trembling from head to toes, looking at her aunt. Upon hearing so much disturbance the other relatives went to the bedroom and were stunned at seeing such a scene. One of them fainted right away and fell like a sac of potatoes causing a big noise. After recomposing from the impact they approached the elderly woman who seemed confused and weak, speaking meaningless words. In spite of walking with half-steps, they helped the dead woman returning to her coffin and accommodated her inside. Then they closed the lid almost with violence and before she could leave again or before she could strike the wood with her knuckles, they sealed it with a hammer and several nails. Without hesitation they raised the heavy box on their shoulders and carried it to the cemetery before the coming of dawn. The next day, without pompous ceremonies, they also buried the corps of the widowed businessman, who had died victim of a sudden cerebral stroke while escaping from his house. The niece could not stop screaming, lost her wits forever and was admitted to a mental hospital, which existed in the *Barrios Altos*, near the great Wall of Lima, for the rest of her life.

The four Republicans came before midnight to start the vigil of Anselmo. They placed themselves at the four corners of the coffin and adopted the military position, illuminated by the powerful funeral lamps. They were wearing their Civil War uniforms. Ivan recited one of the best poems of Miguel Hernández, *Winds of Town.* The next day, when time came to leave for the cemetery, the Republicans and several friends lifted the casket and placed it over their shoulders. They slowly walked down the short staircase and went through the streets of Quirio, singing old songs from the Spanish Civil War era.

21

THE ATTEMPTS OF MANUELITA

The idea of vindication began growing in Manuelita's mind almost immediately after her father died. Her hatred was so intense that she wanted to capture Klaus, tie him down, beat him with a stick and place the electroshock pads on his face, his eyes and his genitalia until she could smell the smoke of burnt flesh. She desired to immerse his head in icy water so he would know the despair of a person who is being tortured. She wished she could sink an ax in his head so that his two halves would fall to the sides still with his eyes hanging from their sockets. Other days, she longed to slowly emasculate him even if he would scream and wail, in German, like a coyote. Her strongest yearning was to see him dying, convulsing, foaming from his mouth, with his eyes looking up to heaven as she had seen a neighbor doing when he shot his own head with an old carbine. At that point, Ivan advised her to work as a servant in Klaus's home if she wanted to get a revenge. Once inside, with her black uniform and a white apron, she could do with him whatever she wanted.

"I could never work as a servant, Ivan. I have dignity and honor."

"Just fool him, Manuelita. There is nothing wrong with working as a maid. Every war is an act of deception. To be successful you have to deceive your enemy. Pretend to be his cook and you will have him at your mercy."

Although the sunny mornings made everyone happy, Manuelita felt tormented by the painful memories of the torture and murder of her progenitor. Instead of feeling elated like everyone else, she had to daily bear the sorrow of her tragedy and the pain which seemed endless.

Eventually, Manuelita followed Ivan's advice and looked for employment in Klaus' house. She went for an interview, brought a letter signed by Ivan and she was accepted. Once inside, they assigned her to a small bedroom with a tiny bed and an old trunk. Her duties were helping with the chores of the house. Working as a domestic, she saw him very often picking his nose while reading the newspaper at breakfast time. He constantly complained that the gardener had left some poisonous plants he had asked him to uproot. For him there was nothing like Germany. Everything was perfect over there.

Sometimes she saw him walking through the garden, listening to the birds chirping, tapping his boots with a small black whip and wearing riding breeches although he didn't know how to ride a horse. Whenever she was in his presence and heard him talking with his peculiar accent, she felt her chest being filled with overflowing contempt and wanted to punch him or choke him, to yell at him and insult him for having killed her father; but she contained herself. At that moment she became very pale and thought she was going to faint. She saw twinkling lights circling around her head and felt very dizzy.

When she added a few drops of cyanide in Klaus's cup of coffee, exactly as Ivan had advised her, she felt a sense of relief. Taking a deep breath, Manuelita stirred the contents of the cup with a little spoon and handed it to him maintaining her composure. He was reading the newspaper at that moment and slowly smelled the coffee. He stopped reading and smelled it several times more. He got up making gestures and poured it in the sink.

"This coffee is not fresh," he said. "Give me another one."

Meanwhile he went back to his reading and continued eating his sandwich made with ham and *salsa criolla*.

Disappointed, Manuelita gave him another cup of coffee and comprehended that her first attempt had failed. She was expecting to see him falling, spilling coffee on his shirt and hearing the cup break against the tiles of the floor; but it had not occurred that way.

At dinner, she told Ivan what had happened and he said:

"This *hijo'e puta* has too many lives. His intuition has saved him."

Ivan suggested the use of another weapon. A well-sharpened knife. There is nothing more effective and swift than cold steel to silence a loquacious tyrant. Once the blade penetrates the heart, the victim falls without having any more thoughts or uttering any more words. Ivan gave her the dagger he used during the Civil War and said:

"This knife does not get old. Many of my enemies died by it. Use it with honor."

That night, when everything in the house was quiet, Manuelita went to Klaus's bedroom walking silently. He did not sleep with his wife because his snoring bothered her. Once inside the room, Manuelita passed by the nightstand and saw an old photograph of Hitler in a military uniform. Klaus had left a thick and long pillow in the place where his wife used to sleep. In that way, if someone came to kill him with a machine gun, the shots would pierce the pillow dispersing its feathers; but he would remain alive. In the same manner, if someone would come to kidnap him, as it happened with Eichmann, they would only grab the pillow. Perhaps then, he would jump out of bed and have time to escape through the bathroom window as he had done before in the quarters of the British Intelligence Office in Berlin.

Klaus snored loudly, with exaggeration. It seemed that the walls trembled with his noise. It was his wife, who had sent him to sleep in that room because she could not rest with his disturbing uproar. Behind the head board there was a red banner on a staff, relatively new, with a black swastika inside a white circle.

She moved very slowly towards him, holding the knife. Despite the darkness, she could see that Klaus was sleeping on his back, with his mouth open and his entire body shaking. For a moment, he remained motionless without being able to suck air. Suddenly he made a loud noise, like when someone is choking, and he took a great deep breath in. Then he continued sleeping as usual.

Manuelita approached him with the knife raised high. For a moment, she saw the brightness of the dagger. However, she felt she could not stab him from a standing position. Consequently, she slowly knelt and leaned over him. She was ready to deliver the weapon into the middle of his chest, but she could not do it. Her two trembling hands were holding the knife above her head, but she was unable to bring them down. It was as if an invisible force had paralyzed them. She struggled again to stab the blade through him, but she could not do it. She remembered the gaping wound on her father's cheekbone and felt angry. At that moment, Klaus stopped snoring and whispered in his dream:

"*Vorsicht!*" (Be careful!)

Then he continued sleeping. Manuelita did not want to think of what would happen if Klaus could wake up at that moment and discover that she was about to stab him. She had no doubt that Klaus would take her knife away, kill her and cut her into small pieces. She stood up and left the room hurriedly with her hands still raised. Only when she reached her bedroom and sat on her bed, she noticed that her arms stiffness was gone. Her hands also became loose. She placed the dagger on the nightstand, laid down on her bed and sobbed silently.

The next day she told Ivan what had happened. Manuelita blamed herself for being incapable of avenging her father. "These hands are so shaky, so weak, so worthless," she said. "I was paralyzed! Can you believe that? I'm a despicable woman. I'm not a good daughter!"

Eating a *tamal*, wrapped in a banana leaf, Ivan advised her to try again, but this time with his revolver. He drew his Smith & Wesson .32 and handed it to her.

"This is a gem," he said. "You can take it with you wherever you go. It is not heavy. It does not bother you. Now it is well-oiled. Beware of the trigger. A little pressure on it and the shot will come out. This can't fail. Tonight when you enter his room, you aim and you shoot. That's all you have to do. Don't think about anything else. Remember. You come in, you aim and you shoot. That's it."

At nightfall, Manuelita waited again for everyone to go to bed. She herself could not close her eyes due to the apprehension and to her disturbing thoughts. She had never wanted to kill anyone; but now she had to do it. She meditated about what would happen next. She recalled her father and sobbed. She asked for his forgiveness because she did not rescue him in time. She blamed herself for allowing her father to be tortured in that way and accepted the idea that he would be happy after knowing what she had done.

Upon hearing the snoring in the adjacent room, Manuelita came out silently from her chamber and recalled Ivan's advice. "Enter, aim and shoot."

She came into his bedroom placing her feet softly on the ground, trying to avoid any noise. She stood in front of Klaus holding the revolver with her two hands and aimed at his head. She hoped to see his face bleeding within the next few seconds. She began to sweat profusely and the tip of her weapon trembled. The shot did not come out. Her whole body became sticky. She sweated from her forehead, her back and her hands. She became afraid and felt nauseated. Manuelita was about to carry out the execution of a heinous torturer, an unrepentant war criminal. Taking several deep breaths to calm herself, she listened to the snoring of Klaus and heard the ticking of the clock on the dresser; but she could not shoot. The thought that Klaus could wake up at that moment and find the gun pointing at his face terrified her. She was convinced that Klaus would take away the revolver and shoot her instead. Manuelita felt her throat becoming dry. Her palpitations intensified and she felt them strongly in her chest and especially in her head. From the glowing numbers on the alarm clock, she knew that it was two o'clock in the morning. The image of Hitler on the night desk seemed to stare at her. She made another effort and aimed at Klaus's face. Her entire body trembled; but the shot did not come out.

At that moment Klaus, unexpectedly, raised and sat up in his bed. Panic swept over Manuelita's entire body and she stopped breathing. She thought Klaus had discovered her. She felt that her legs gave way and that she was fainting.

"Oh, fuck! He woke up!," she exclaimed inside her mind. Frightened, almost stumbling, but still aiming at Klaus, she stepped back and leaned against the wall with her legs trembling. She felt that she was losing consciousness.

Klaus was not fully awake either. His eyes were half opened. He sat at the edge of the bed. The garden light entering through the window illuminated his face. He looked like a zombie, like someone who is half-dead and half-alive. He said a few words in German and made a motion in the air as if fixing an invisible microphone with his hands. He tapped on it with his fingers to confirm that it was functioning. Then he gently rubbed his chin. He stood up as if he was on a podium and began to give a speech to a non-existent audience with a feeble voice.

With a serious face, lifting his chin and turning his furious eyes from one side to the other, he raised his voice and spoke with a lot of energy. It was a perfect imitation of Hitler. He spoke and made gestures as his Führer used to make during his famous speeches. Klaus moved his fist, from his chest to the front, several times and gestured angrily. Histrionically, he lifted his two hands above his head and lowered them slowly, down to his chest, while still speaking, opening his mouth widely and looking at the ceiling. Then he raised a hand and moved it forward, shaking it, as if pointing to someone in the audience. Suddenly he ceased talking. Appearing angry he placed a hand over his upper lip to fix an invisible mustache that was falling off.

Astonished, Manuelita continued pointing at him. Nevertheless, Klaus seemed to be unaware of her presence. Looking through her, as if she was not there, he made an involuntary movement and slightly touched the tip of the gun with a finger; but she moved it away quickly and felt that her heart had stopped from fear.

The speech ended. His face blushed after becoming aware of what he had done. He greeted his listeners raising an open hand over his shoulder. Then he stretched his arm forward, in a Nazi salute, and sat at the edge of his bed accommodating his imaginary mustache.

Manuelita came near him and placed the tip of her gun close to his face, but it seemed that Klaus could not see her despite having his eyes open. She made an effort to shoot. Her hand trembled awkwardly as well as her entire body. Her finger did not obey. It was as if the trigger had jammed. She felt that her hands were sweating and that her gun had become too big and heavy and was falling from her hands.

Klaus leaned back in his bed, pulled the sheet over himself, closed his eyes and began to snore. Manuelita furiously, lowered her hands and left the room in a hurry. She heard footsteps approaching the bedroom. So, she stepped back and leaned against the wall. It was Klaus' wife standing at the door. After seeing that her husband was snoring loudly and that everything was in order, she turned around and walked away. Manuelita waited until she entered her bedroom and shut the door.

Then she walked towards her own chamber. Once there, she could not sleep. She was too angry with herself. She blushed and bit her lip. She wept for a while.

The next day the Spanish Republican, smoking his reed pipe, explained to her:

"It's because you are not a killer, *niña yuntera*. Your soul is too noble. You have not been on the battlefront either, where killing is a necessity. You could never kill anyone. Don't blame yourself. You are not for this. You are too good to be a murderer."

22

THE DROWNING OF IVAN

The Quirio *Canal* provides water for the local population through the wells constructed along its sides. During the rainy season, the water from the Andes overflows into it. People drown in the Canal. When someone disappears, the police close the river gate and the Canal becomes dry. After this, the drowned individual usually appears at the bottom.

Klaus heard the sound of the water rushing by. The smell was unmistakable. It reminded him of the Rhône River. His assistants removed the black hood from Ivan's head and tied a large stone to his belt. Against his will they wrapped the rope around his waist several times and made knots. The tightness annoyed Ivan. They made him sit at the rocky edge of the Canal. Klaus had the impression that someone was singing a song by Leo Marini in the distance. Still he could not conclude whether it was his imagination or if someone was really singing.

The detectives lifted then threw the big stone into the water and the heavy weight dragged Ivan, who fell making a big splash. Klaus held him above the surface pulling him by his hair. Ivan spat out the water that had entered his mouth and felt a sharp burning sensation inside his nose. Klaus pushed his head vigorously into the water. Smiling, he pulled him up; Ivan gasped for air and opened his mouth widely. Water was trickling down his face.

"Don't you like it, republican?" Klaus asked.

He pushed him down again; waited for a minute, calculating. Then he pulled him out.

"I want the names of the four Republicans," he said.

He pushed him once more. Then he pulled him afloat. Ivan thought he was seeing General Franco, standing at the side of Klaus, looking at him calmly with his fists on his hip and his legs set apart. Also the three Nationalists, with their somber faces and one knee on the ground, stared at him in silence. At that time, Ivan began to recite a known poem of Miguel Hernández:

> *"When I die, I want to die*
> *With my head held high..."*

Klaus submerged him into the water and everybody heard bubbles bursting on the surface. He waited for a while and then pulled him out.

"I want the names of the four Republicans!," Klaus screamed with his characteristic accent.

Ivan, blinking his eyes, continued with the poem:

> *"Dead and twenty times dead,*
> *my mouth against the grass*
> *I will have my teeth clenched*
> *and determined my chin ..."*

Klaus pushed him down and his assistants heard the bubbles bursting again. Klaus brought him up. At this time, Ivan felt that he could not see the image of Klaus well and could not hear his voice. Rather he began to see Franco and the Nationalists with more clarity. He even noted that one of them was using a toothpick. At that moment he heard the song that terrified him most. As if someone had raised the volume of a record player to its loudest, he heard a chorus of powerful *staccato* voices singing with great clarity:

> *"Facing the sun with the new shirt*
> *That you in red embroidered yesterday...*
> *Death will find me and*
> *I will not see you again..."*

Overwhelmed by panic, in a counterpoint, Ivan continued his recitation:

> *"Singing I wait for death*
> *For there are nightingales that*
> *sing over the rifles*
> *in the midst of the battlefield."*

At that moment Klaus pushed his head down saying: "You better die, you shitty Republican!"

Klaus was convinced that the tortured one would not survive. The Republican's body would appear the next day drowned in some bend of the waterway. The police will order to dry the Canal until Ivan would appear sitting at the bottom, leaning against the wall of stones, with his eyes looking straight forward and the water covering him, up to his chest. Nobody could escape with a rock tied around the body.

Overcome by terror Ivan lifted his hand out of the water and tried to grab Klaus's hand, but he made efforts to keep him below the surface. Ivan's fingers struggled desperately. Then they weakened, became inert and sank into the water. Klaus kept him under the surface for a few more seconds and then let him go. He tried to see in the darkness; but he could only distinguish the nearby surface and heard the sound of the current.

After Klaus released him, Ivan continued floating with all his extremities hanging loose. Almost immediately, in the darkness, Ivan emerged forcefully from the water, like when a whale comes out from the ocean. He appeared with his eyes widely open, sucking air through his mouth with desperation. He still felt numb, with a strong buzzing sound in his ears. He continued moving his hands and legs, and felt the water coming out from his nose. He kept floating, breathing heavily, until he recovered all his senses. Then he plunged in the water again. Embraced the rock and lifted it, kicking his feet, until he came back to the surface. The water current kept dragging him; but he managed to untie the rope and let the stone sink by itself. Then, he grasped the slippery edge of the Canal and climbed up with difficulty, feeling very cold. He remained exhausted and shivering, with his wet clothes and with his ears filled with water, which did not allow him to hear. He lied down on the grass near one of the water wells, smelled the weeds and fell asleep.

.

23

MANUELITA FINDS A LETTER ADDRESSED TO KLAUS

The next morning, while making Klaus's bed, Manuelita straightened the blanket, pulled the sheets tight and covered the pillows with the bed spread. Then she passed a clean cloth over the night desk and rubbed the glass of the alarm clock with the fluorescent numbers. Near Hitler's portrait, she found an envelope addressed to Klaus. She picked it up, opened it and carefully pulled a thin, almost transparent paper. In the upper right corner of the sheet she observed a Nazca Humming Bird silhouette with its parallel wings, printed in light blue color. She read the content:

National Socialist Movement of Northern Peru.
Dear Kamerade:

Heil Hitler!

> *By this letter, I wish to send you the greetings of our National Socialist Movement from this Northern region of Peru. I would also like to take this opportunity to communicate to you a certain situation that should be very much of your*

concern, because it has to do with a serious threat against your physical safety and your life.

My contacts from Argentina and Chile, old S.S. Kamerades, inform me that you have a formidable and dangerous enemy who is planning to travel to Peru to eliminate you. I am referring to the Mayor of Oyonnax, who is still the venerated leader of hundreds of followers who insist on bearing the name of maquis.

The Mayor of Oyonnax, dear kamerade, as you could very well understand, has aged. He is about seventy years old now. However, his intelligence remains as pristine and sharp as ever. The most remarkable thing about him is his physical vigor, which in the opinion of everybody, must be due to the excellent wine of Ain. He drinks it in great amounts before and after every meal.

He is older now, but his warrior impetus, has not changed. He is always threatening an attack on his enemies. His power over his followers is absolute. It is enough for him to move a finger and his men, automatically, adopt the position of attention, and present their British sub machine guns, indicating their readiness to annihilate any of the Mayor's adversaries or any enemy of France.

He still rides his old BMW R 75 motorcycle, which he captured during the war. Some parts of it are rusty. It makes intolerable noise and breaks down frequently on the road, in obvious need for a mechanic. However the Mayor knows how to make his engine run and work as if it was new.

His vigor is admirable; despite his obvious senility, he has changed wives three times since you were in the Gestapo office of Lyon. The last one is a young maiden, so tender that she seems to be a great grand daughter rather than a wife. She has shown to be a very faithful and devoted spouse and she watches over him at all times.

Even when she is with child, she puts a blanket over his shoulders, so he will not get sick. She also keeps an eye on his diet and she is the one pouring the good wine of Ain in his glass, before and after each meal, or when the Mayor wishes it.

His followers, who number in the hundreds, are in very good physical and mental condition. Although some have passed away, those who are still alive are in a good shape for combat. They exercise and train daily in the mountains of Ain. They have become experts in guerrilla warfare to such a degree that it is common thought, that if they were to fight, no Army could defeat them. Besides, they have encouraged their sons and grandchildren to enroll. All of them have become such a powerful force, and it is believed, that the French Resistance is invincible and more powerful that ever.

You should know, kamerade, that the Mayor of Oyonnax has been looking for you for a long time. Recently, he learned that you were hiding in the city of Lima, near the suburbs of Chaclacayo and Santa Maria. The last report I received from Paraguay, indicated that they were already in Lima, and that they could visit you now at any time.

He keeps telling everybody that he will capture you as the Mossad did with Adolf Eichmann in Buenos Aires. The difference is that he is not planning to bring you back to France. Instead, he has decided to execute you as soon as he finds you. He insists in the fact that you have been trialed and sentenced by a French Tribunal already. The only action pending is your execution. He is ready to do that. As you may recall, the French Tribunal found you guilty of the torture and assassination of forty-two French Jewish citizens, the deportation of other six hundred and fifty innocent victims, including the fifty-five Jewish children of Izieu to the concentration camps of Ravensbrük and Auchswitz.

After they find you, they will make you stand at the center of your garden and the one hundred followers will shoot you with their machine guns, from all sides, at the same time, until all their bullets are finished. You will not have a summary trial. Can you imagine a hundred maquis shooting at you at the same time? You will end up with more holes in your body than the old sieve of a potato picker. They will convert you into a big mass of flesh, completely unrecognizable. Chopped and minced, like ground beef, ready to be cooked as a Kohl Rolle. (Cabbage roll)

For this reason, I have taken the liberty of writing to you, being an old kamerade of mine, and warn you about this dangerous situation. I would recommend you to leave this country immediately and go to more welcoming lands such as Bolivia, Argentina or Brazil. Or perhaps Paraguay. These nations have been so generous to us, the ones who pursue the return of the Third Reich as the only salvation for the entire world.

If I receive any other information, I will gladly communicate it to you immediately if you let me know your whereabouts.

Hoping that Nazi Germany will return soon to its previous glory, I raise my hand and say:

Heil Hitler!

We, the servers of his Majesty, the Führer.

Colonel Fritz Schuster Müller

Commandant General to the Central Detachment. Gamma cell. Province of Tumbez. Northern Peru.

Once she finished reading the letter Manuelita's face illuminated. She meditated and thought she had found a good idea. "As Ivan said, a word can be more lethal than a gun." She did not need a dagger or a Smith & Wesson .32. She decided to write another letter addressed to Klaus. Very carefully, she wrote over another piece of paper.

Mr. Butcher of Lyon:

It is a pleasure to announce to you that we the Justice Seekers of France, the ones who rigorously chastise crimes with strict discipline, are here in Lima at this moment.

We know where you reside and we want to let you know that we will be at your place tomorrow at 8 o'clock in the morning. I have to tell you that you will have to prepare breakfast for one hundred people and have ready a gallon of high quality red wine.

When you hear the sounds of my motorcycle, you will know that I am there and that we have surrounded your house. You will not have a chance to escape.

Please, be happy. We have, at last, found you.

The Mayor of Oyonnax and his One Hundred maquis.

Long live France!

Manuelita folded the letter and placed it inside an envelope addressed to Klaus. She left the correspondence on the night desk, next to the black and white photograph, and left the room.

24

ESCAPE TO BOLIVIA

During those agitated days, Klaus hung a sign on his office door that said "Section IVB4". This intrigued his subordinates who asked him:

"But, Colonel. If we don't have Section III or Section V, how is it possible that you want to have an office called Section IV?"

"That does not matter. This was the way we named our Gestapo office in Berlin. It was the Intelligence Service. Do you understand? It has always been Section IVB4. And this is the way it is going to be."

He also was planning to hang Hitler's picture in his office like the one he had at the Terminus Hotel. When his men found him with a hammer and a nail in his hands, they told him that in Lima he had to hang a picture of Francisco Bolognesi, laying down, aiming his revolver at one of his enemies. Or a picture of Admiral Miguel Grau, with his arms crossed and a foot raised over a spool of rope. He answered:

"I am a German. If this is the case, I will not hang anything."

He left the picture leaning on the wall; but he did not last in that office for too long either.

When Klaus found Manuelita's letter on his night desk, he remained speechless for a few minutes. He was shocked to learn about the arrival of the Mayor of Oyonnax, riding his motorcycle and being followed by his one hundred maquis. The note informed him that they would arrive at 8 o'clock the following morning. He did not think twice. Immediately he prepared his luggage, placed it in the trunk of his jeep and left home. He drove through the streets, towards his Miraflores bungalow. He picked up Kassandra, who was somnolent and dressed with a *poncho* and a *chullo* on her head. She didn't forget to bring a cassette with the songs of Bienvenido Granda. Despite the darkness, they left Lima and took the road going to Arequipa and Puno, in an effort to cross the Bolivian border that same night.

The other powerful reason he fled to Bolivia was that he had received a subpoena to appear in court to answer certain questions related to the murder investigation of his neighbor, Luis Banchero Rossi, a Peruvian industrialist. The judicial authorities suspected that Klaus had committed the crime, but could not prove anything. When they ordered his capture he had already crossed the border with Bolivia.

Several days later, after re-establishing himself in the city of La Paz, he read in the newspapers that a squad of construction workers had found the human remains of Martin Bormann in Berlin. They had found them where the *Invalidienstrasse* crossed the railroad tracks. The oral X-rays delivered by his dentist, Dr. Hugo Blaschke, had helped in the identification.

While Kassandra was in bed, recovering from severe mountain sickness, Klaus read that after Hitler's suicide, his most faithful companions decided to abandon their shelter in an attempt to escape Berlin on the night of May 1, 1945. Advancing in a small group, under the leadership of Martin Bormann, they decided to use the underground train tunnel until they emerged at the *Friedrichstrasse* station. Once on the street they observed that the city of Berlin had become a ferocious and deadly battlefield.

There were explosions and gunfire everywhere. They tried to cross the *Weidendammer* Bridge protected by several German tanks. After they reached *Ziegelstrasse*, the Russian artillery attacked the tanks with a *Katyusha* missile and destroyed them. The explosions affected Bormann who became confused, bewildered and unable to hear for a few moments.

After recovering, the stout Bormann, who had signed Hitler's political will and had been one of the witnesses of his wedding to the nagging Eva Braun, discovered that his ears were buzzing fiercely. He also realized that his strength had abandoned him and that he was very sick.

Staggering, Martin Bormann walked together with Arthur Axmann, a leader of the Hitlerian Youth and Dr. Ludwig Stumpfegger, Hitler's physician. After the assassination attempt lead by Lieutenant Colonel Claus Schenk Graf von Stauffenberg, he took care of the *Führer's* lesions. Dr. Stumpfegger was an orthopedic surgeon who, by that time, was becoming famous. His growing prestige was due to his attempts to transplant coccyx bones from one prisoner to another.

They advanced westward by the train tracks with the intention of arriving at the *Lehrter* station, in a long trip that ran parallel to the Spree river. After an exhausting journey, walking over the tracks, they arrived at the station and realized that the explosions and shootings did not allow them to advance any further. Going out into the streets at that moment would have been deadly. However, Axman, stronger and without feeling any fatigue, with his red face covered by cinder, decided to continue escaping and left his two companions.

Bormann concluded that it was too late to escape from Berlin and decided to do what he had not dared to accomplish in front of his beloved *Führer*. Completely out of breath and extremely exhausted, they laid down on the ground, one next to each other. Bormann, still with twinkling lights moving around his head, took out from his pocket a glass capsule containing cyanide and offered it to the bone specialist. Looking at the tip of his black boots, Bormann took another capsule and said with labored breathing:

"Farewell, Doktor Stumpfegger, tailbone transplanter."

Clicking his heels clumsily, the tall Physician in Nazi uniform answered:

"Farewell, *Obersturmbanführer* Bormann, shadow and right hand of our Almighty Führer."

Still listening to the explosions and the rattling shots of the machine guns, they bit the glass capsules, gathered the liquid with their tongues and swallowed it. Almost instantaneously, they became motionless.

Axmann, meanwhile, returned after meeting a Russian patrol, which fired at him mercilessly and almost killed him. Next to the station, where the *Invalidienstrasse* crossed over the tracks of the railroad, he found Bormann and Stumpfegger. They were apparently dead, with their eyes open, as if they were contemplating the cloud that was passing in front of the moon.

The leader of the Hitlerian Youth escaped from Berlin and managed to find shelter in the Bavarian mountains. Several months later, the U.S. Army Military Police found him in a house, drinking from a tall glass of beer while listening to one of Hitler's discourses. After breaking down the door, the police officers handcuffed him and took him away. When they were leaving the cottage, the phonograph was still playing the Munich Speech very loudly.

In the middle of the chaos, the horror and the libertinism in which Berlin sank during the following weeks, nobody found the remains of Bormann or Doctor Stumpfegger. Little by little, the dust and the garbage brought by the wind covered their bodies. Their uniforms and boots also disintegrated.

A decade later, a noble rodent, in search of a meal for its offspring, stopping and advancing, came near the white skull of Bormann. Raising its delicate snout, he explored and made rounds inside the socket of one eye. Moving its whiskers gracefully, the small animal climbed over the top of the skull and sniffed the air. Then, climbing down, it walked quickly over the row of teeth where a few glass particles appeared near a silver filling. The rodent descended to the breastbone and jumped down onto the curved, Nazi lumbar spine. Then, sniffing the soil the delicate rodent went away, in search of food for its offspring. Martin Bormann's bones remained undiscovered for the next three decades until a group of construction workers found them in the same military position he adopted when he decided to ingest cyanide.

25

BACK TO LYON

Finally, in 1983, after the persistent and diligent work of Serge and Beate Klarsfeld, the Miterrand government requested his extradition to France. Likewise, the new democratic government of Bolivia considered that it was time to send him back to the place of his crimes. They arrested him for fraud during the process of immigration and deported him in a private plane. During the long journey, passing through the clouds of the Atlantic Ocean, he remained motionless and speechless. There was no *kamerade* to talk to while enjoying with a glass of beer, as had occurred during his initial trip to Argentine, on the steamship *Corrientes*. There was no General Auerbach, who could entertain him with his magic tricks and escape performances. He did not mention the long and hairy ears of the detectives of *El Fronton Island*, nor could he call *Leerer Schädel* to the agents who were flying with him. The times of his alleged and false superiority had ended. Kassandra, unable to adjust to the altitude of La Paz, had returned to Lima. The beautiful Cuban dancer, drinking *mojitos* and *pisco-sours,* ended up working for the rest of her life in the bustling nightclubs of the city. She enjoyed the pleasures of sex, alcohol and drugs until her last day. Once the airplane arrived to the city of Lyon, the French authorities interned him in the Montluc Prison.

Meanwhile, Field Marshall Rudolf Hess remained interned as the only inmate of the Spandau military jail in Berlin. They confined him there in 1946, after a Military Court in Nuremberg sentenced him to life imprisonment. Everything began for Hess on May of 1941, when he climbed, with his boundless megalomania and a parachute on his back, into a Messerschmitt ME-110. After putting his goggles on and tying a light blue silk scarf around his neck, he initiated a flight from Augsburg to England, without any guide or help. With no navigation charts, he flew by intuition moving among clouds and turbulence. After a long trip, listening to his engine roaring, he parachuted and let his airship, with a black swastika on its tail, crash near a Glasgow mountain. Making gestures of pain, because he had injured his foot during the fall, he announced to a Scottish peasant that he had an important message for King Henry the VIII.

During the cross-examination done by the British officers, he informed them that he was the legendary Rudolf Hess, second only to Hitler. He insisted on being the one who had written the manuscript of *Mein Kampf*, while the *Führer* had spent all that time kicking an empty bottle and talking nonsense inside their cell. He added that he had come to England to meet with the Ghost of the Castle of Elsinore and requested to be brought to his presence immediately. He wanted to talk about world peace. After Hess demonstrated other signs of mental instability, the English authorities considered him insane. For that reason, they retained him as a prisoner of war in the Tower of London. There, in a solitary cell, accompanied only by a faithful rat, which enjoyed listening to him, he spent his time reciting, with a slight German accent, fragments of his favorite play *Macbeth*:

> *"Is this a dagger which I see before me,*
> *The handle toward my hand?*
> *Come, let me clutch thee!*

I have thee not, and yet I see thee still.
Are thou not, fatal vision, sensible
To feeling as to sight? Or art thou but
A dagger of the mind, a false creation..."

The Nuremberg Court had sentenced him to strict solitary confinement. Therefore, in the Spandau prison he was not allowed to recite dramatic pieces anymore. That correctional institution remained open only to take care of Rudolf Hess with an expense for the German government of 850,000 marks per year. For vigilance, the four Allied Powers had to provide a team composed of an officer and thirty-seven soldiers every month.

The Spandau Military Prison was an impressive building constructed in the XIX century. It gave the impression of being a medieval fortress. There was a thick brick wall and an electrified fence around the penitentiary. Smoking or speaking to anyone was forbidden. They did not allow the guards to communicate with Hess. Before entering the building, they had to search everyone, to prevent the smuggling of cigarettes or photographic cameras.

They let him walk in the garden for two hours exactly, in the mornings and in the evenings. He strolled endlessly around the penal institution. From the distance, he looked like a very happy clown, lifting his arms and knees to preserve his strength and stamina. Sometimes, he gallantly marched alone in front of a watchtower, as if he was in one of the *Wehrmacht* parades, giving orders in loud voice and saluting with an invisible sword to an imaginary tribune. Other days, raising a hand in the Nazi style, he greeted personalities who, in his mind, had come to visit him. One Spring morning he saw *Reichsführer* Heinrich Himmler walking on the grass. With his black uniform, his bright glasses and a great smile, the top officer in charge of the concentration camps advanced slowly towards him. Alarmed Hess asked him.

"Are you a remembrance of my mind, a false creation or a real being?"

"I am the real thing," answered Himmler, smiling and stomping one foot over the ground.

When Hess, very moved, almost crying, with a knot in his throat, clicked his heels and lifted his arm to give a Nazi salute, the image vanished.

Another day, when he was doing frog jumps across the garden, he unexpectedly saw Field Marshall Friedrich Paulus coming towards him, from the opposite direction, also doing frog jumps. Hess, very surprised, stopped jumping. Breathing heavily, with his hands on his waste, he observed his visitor with great expectation and said:

"Oh, mein Gott! Marshal Paulus!" (Oh, my God! Marshal Paulus!)

The Marshal smiled at him and with mocking eyes replied:

"Ist es nicht Fräulein Hess?" (Isn't it Miss Hess?)

The visitor was dressed with the same thick winter coat he had worn during the siege of Stalingrad. When they were in front of each other, still in the squatting position, Hess, speechless, noticed the fine drops of perspiration on the pale forehead and the labored breathing of his drop-in company. Hess immediately stood up, clicked his heels and adopted a military position. When he mentioned the Marshal's name again, the image faded.

One year later, he saw Field Marshal Erwin Rommel with the same leather coat he had used in El Alamein. With dusty face, dry lips and binoculars around his neck, he was coming towards him. They greeted each other in the Nazi fashion and even sat down on the grass to chat a little. At one moment, still with the goggles over his visor cap, Rommel lifted his binoculars, seriously looked at the Russian guards of the Prison watchtower and calmly said with great assertiveness.

"I could blow them up with one single shot."

At that moment, Rommel became very serious and turned toward Hess. Silently the Field Marshall stared at him for a few seconds. Then, very coldly, he said:

"Wir hatten, Hitler zu töten ... Es gab keinen anderen Weg..." ("We had to kill Hitler... There was no other way...")

Upon hearing this Hess blushed and became offended. When he wanted to reply angrily the image disappeared.

Rudolf Hess spent most of his time in his cell, constantly reminiscing the moments of glory he had shared with Hitler. He recalled him giving a speech in a small Munich bar when a rabble of political adversaries attacked them with sticks and bottles, wounding his head and giving him a black eye. He also recollected when he wrote, inside their cell, what Hitler dictated during the preparation of the *Mein Kampf* manuscript. Occasionally, he heard in his mind the roaring of the crowds and the unending applause of the public when he introduced Hitler. He remembered the screams of the audience, *"Führer! Führer! Führer!"* and the white handkerchiefs waving in the air incessantly. Then he only perceived the silence, the chirps of the little birds, the fallen leaves and the quiet prison trees. The walls of his cell had the numerous marks he had made to count the days and the years that had passed after they locked him up. It also had the death skull image he drew as soon as he arrived.

At the end, after living through several decades in complete isolation, speaking only to the birds and to imaginary beings, Hess turned into an elderly, hoary and blind man. By that time, he walked with tremulous steps, inclined forward and resting on a cane; but still believing firmly, that he had been born in Egypt, at the foot of a pyramid, among nursing camels, in order to save humanity. He was supposed to be the last Pharaoh of the Third Reich.

On August 17, 1987, the world knew that Rudolf Hess had passed away at the age of 93. Apparently, strange and unknown visitors had strangled him inside his own cell. One month earlier, in July of 1987, after a long judicial process, a French Court had sentenced the Butcher of Lyon to life imprisonment. The order was to incarcerate him in the same cells of the Montluc Prison, where he had tortured, electro shocked and killed, with a shot to the head, many of his innocent victims. He had to live with their terrifying and vengeful ghosts, who appeared at night, accusing him of what he had done, insulting him and threatening to kill him.

The warden did not give him any special consideration or treatment. Instead, it was necessary to move him from cell to cell, at unexpected hours of the night, because there were rumors that someone was coming to strangle him inside the prison. The one who complained most was the exchange prisoner who had to occupy his cell.

"Hey! How about me? Suppose they choke me instead of that Butcher! Get me out of here! Now!"

"Shut up! Go back to sleep!," shouted someone else from another cell.

Klaus mentioned repeatedly that it was the Mayor of Oyonnax, who had threatened to end his life. He had promised to come to Montluc, riding his motorcycle, accompanied by a large number of his followers, to execute him. By that time, no one listened to him anymore.

At the end, when he was agonizing in his cell, awakening and fainting, he said.

"Alles hat ein Ende." (Everything has an end.)

Afterwards, he remained quiet, ready for his burial. The only thing he took with him to his sepulcher was his bronze ring with the image of a death skull sculpted on its bezel, and the letters *S.D.* inscribed on the side of its hoop.

THE END

ABOUT THE AUTHOR

Manuel Lasso, a Peruvian novelist, short story writer and playwright, studied Literature at the City College of New York, where he became a winner of the Floral Games in the narrative category. His work has been published in magazines and newspapers from Europe and America and has readers in five continents. Visit his blog http://manuellasso.blogspot.com or follow him on Twitter @Manuel_Lasso.

13698973R00090

Printed in Great Britain
by Amazon.co.uk, Ltd.,
Marston Gate.